FUTURE
FAITH
CHURCHES

DON POSTERSKI
& GARY NELSON

FUTURE
FAITH
CHURCHES

Reconnecting with
the Power of the Gospel
for the 21st Century

 WOOD LAKE BOOKS

Editor: James Taylor
Editorial colleagues: Chuck Ferguson, Joan Morin
Cover and interior design: Margaret Kyle
Consulting art director: Robert MacDonald
Cover people photos: James Taylor
Nebula image: This image was created with support to Space Telescope
Science Institute, operated by the Association of Universities for Research
in Astronomy, Inc., from NASA contract NAS5-26555, and is reproduced
with permission from Aura/STScI. Digital renditions of images produced
byAURA/STScI are obtainable royalty-free. The use of this image in no
way implies the endorsement by AURA/STScI or by any AURA/STScI
employee of the material contained in this book.

Canadian Cataloguing in Publication Data
Posterski, Donald C., 1942 –
Future faith churches

Includes bibliographical references.
ISBN 1-55145-098-4

1. Church and the world. 2. Mission of the church.
3. Christianity – Canada. I. Nelson, Gary Vincent. II. Title.
BR115.W6P67 1997 261'.1'0971 C97-910697-4

Published by
Wood Lake Books Inc., Winfield, British Columbia

Printing 9 8 7 6 5 4 3 2 1

Printed in Canada by
Transcontinental Printing, Peterborough, Ontario

CONTENTS

Foreword **7**

Preface **11**

Introduction **17**

The Heritage of Future Faith Churches **23**

Discerning the Soul of Future Faith Churches **57**

Discerning the Soul of Future Faith Leaders **83**

Strategies for Future Faith Leaders **101**

Energizing Future Faith Churches **121**

Non-Negotiables for Future Faith Churches **167**

Faith Fit for the Future **193**

Appendices **229**

Endnotes **245**

FOREWORD

You will enjoy this book. *Future Faith Churches* is about churches and ideas that come alive. It's about churches who practice soul care and social care; they love God and they have compassion for people. Don Posterski and Gary Nelson challenge us to consider the example and experience of some of the most effective churches in Canada. These 14 churches have combined the strands of evangelism, social action, church growth, and strong leadership to create the fabric for a worshiping community that is life-changing.

In discussions about the church, two questions emerge: What's possible? And who cares? On the matter of what is possible, the authors review the styles, approaches, and attitudes of "Future Faith" congregations. Then they follow the trail of each church's ambitious course. Without apology, these churches love God and love their neighbors. They practice a holistic Christian faith that is biblical, relevant, and attractive both to their communities and to the wider world.

The evidence collected in this book embraces Pentecostals, Catholics, mainline, and evangelical Protestants, as well as ethnic churches. The authors are wise enough to observe that one approach won't work. Genuinely effective churches read their community, listen to their constituency, respect the authority of Christ, and discern the leading of the Holy Spirit. Many helpful principles emerge in this book, but churches that practice both soul care and social care know the necessary balance between the hard and soft elements of vital faith. The principles may be similar, but each church has a unique vision and plan.

On the matter of "Who cares?" it becomes obvious that the leaders, both clergy and lay people, of these Future Faith churches care very deeply. Often out of their brokenness has come a new understanding and a common vision of what it means to be an effective worshiping and witnessing community. A similar vulnerability and passion develops among their church members as well. These leaders cut new ground by inviting and consulting rather than coercing and dominating. The result is a Gospel that meets parishes and congregations where they succeed and fail on a daily basis. Here is an antidote to those who say the church is broken and ineffective.

This book will challenge your comfort zones. Cultural and religious pluralism is not something to be destroyed, but rather an opportunity to show the graciousness and relevance of real Christianity. This latter proposition is especially important if the church is to be an effective witness in our increasingly pluralistic society. It's high time that real Christians steer a midway course between those who want to attack every other religion and those who accept everything as simply another way to reach the same destination.

This book is a wake-up call for denominational leadership. More and more evidence is emerging to support the reality that new life in virtually every denomination is coming from the local congregations. Any denominational leadership that ignores this trend will pay a heavy price in both growth and effectiveness.

The place of compassion and generosity is another central feature of effective Canadian churches. There is compelling survey work that reveals the attitudes Future Faith Christians have towards issues of faith and practice. In fact our research at World Vision shows that regular church going Christians are the predominant supporters of most charity work on behalf of the poor. Not only are their attitudes different, but what they give is more generous. Inviting more Canadians to follow Jesus is critical for the work of charities across this country.

Posterski and Nelson push it even further by saying that Future Faith Christians reflect an attitude of generosity around many belief and practice issues. This is an important discovery when many previous commentators have observed that there is little difference between Christians and non-Christians in practice and belief.

It's wonderful to know that people who take inviting others into the faith seriously, also have compassion for the poor.

Christianity can be both relevant and truthful in a contemporary Canada that travels a mostly secular highway. These fourteen churches have clear faith non-negotiables. They know who they are, where they are, and how they should relate to the big issues. The banks of their communal river have been built, but there is still plenty of room for the water to flow. They have learned how to separate the big things from the little things and they respond to them accordingly. Just maybe we are drawing closer to the day when Pentecostals and mainline Protestants, evangelicals, Roman Catholics, and Orthodox will kneel and work together before a Jesus whose heart is broken by the ruptured souls and the physical misery of this marvelous tragic creation.

Theologian Karl Rahner once said, "The number one cause of atheism is Christians. Those who proclaim God with their mouths and deny him with their lifestyles are what an unbelieving world finds simply unbelievable."

Here is an answer to Rahner's criticism. These are churches which match words with deeds, and embrace a holistic Christian faith. Future Faith churches in Canada are doing just that. They invite followers of Jesus to link their inward journey with the responsibility to help others.

We need more churches like this. The future of Christian faith in Canada depends on it.

Dave Toycen
President, World Vision Canada

PREFACE

We (Gary and Don) write this book with an unapologetic
love for the church. We do so with an awareness that "love is
patient and kind, love keeps no record of wrongs, love protects and trusts and hopes." Accordingly, we also confess our
frustrations with aspects of the same church we seek to love.
Our perspectives are especially affected by the realization that
the two of us are a part of the church God desires to enable.
Still, we are more hopeful today than ever before. After studying and sensing the spirit of the people and clergy in the 14
Future Faith Churches that are the focus of this book, we are
convinced that God plans impressive futures for Canadian
churches.

DON'S ACKNOWLEDGMENTS

Over the past 15 years, I have been mentored by several competent and creative researchers. Reg Bibby has distinguished
himself as the premier sociologist and media spokesperson
in religion in Canada and I have benefited greatly from his
input and friendship. Irwin Barker, formerly from The An-

gus Reid Group in Winnipeg, helped me understand the power of ministry models. This current project included good counsel from Kirk Hadaway in designing the interview guides. Andrew Grenville from The Angus Reid Group in Toronto offered insight and permission to use the national comparative data included in this book. Rob Burbach added his analytical expertise and interpreted the survey data that substantiates the claim that the Future Faith Churches are, indeed, places that epitomize "high soul care" and "high social care."

A couple of years ago, I received an e-mail from a University of Victoria graduate student named Daryl Thomson. He had just read *Where's a Good Church?* and wondered whether there were any future research projects that might utilize his interest and skills. Arrangements were eventually made for Daryl to spend a mutually beneficial work term with World Vision Canada. He became a competent research assistant and served faithfully as a valued partner on this project.

One of the privileges of my life is to have the opportunity to actualize some of my more feasible ideas. The church relations mandate in my job description as Vice President of National Programs for World Vision Canada made this project important and possible. Important because the same "love God and love your neighbor" gospel practiced by the Future Faith Churches is what World Vision seeks to practice. Possible – because of the resources and personnel support World Vision provided.

Two people in particular extended themselves beyond the boundaries of their job descriptions: Chuck Ferguson served as a literature researcher, first draft writer of Chapter 1, constructive critic, and an in-house editor. His work lifted the level of the final manuscript. Joan Morin is a vocational gift to me. Her administrative support, reminders, and occasional directives are all symbols of her readiness to contribute without being asked. Jim Taylor from Wood Lake Books added his creative editorial skills as well as his competent counsel and personal care.

This book is the tenth that has been published with my name on the cover. My partner for life has patiently and supportively been alongside in all the steps of the journey. Beth, I owe you big time!

One of the delights of this book is having the opportunity to be a voice for others. The pages that follow include a weaving of the insights of 14 dedicated and gifted clergy in Canada. As well, there are scores of discerning statements from over 100 spiritually vibrant lay people. This project would have remained as just an idea if they had not given up their time and offered their cooperation. To everyone involved in the 14 Future Faith Churches, thank you, and may God continue to bless and lead you to set benchmarks for others.

At one point in this project, I remarked to Gary, "There are so many people involved, we will end up writing a book by committee." His response reveals his pastoral perspective: "Don't you mean it will be a book by community?" Part of my motivation for inviting Gary to co-author was to be sure that the end product was grounded in the reality of local church life. As well as keeping us anchored in reality, Gary has contributed significantly – even when he had to endure my drive to have the last word. Gary, your influence is all over this manuscript and I'm grateful.

Don Posterski

GARY'S ACKNOWLEDGMENTS

For the past seven years, I have been able to serve a vibrant and creative congregation of people called First Baptist Church, in Edmonton, Alberta. We have walked together in a process of renewal and revitalization which has not always been easy but always stretching. This unique community of faith provided me a sabbatical of six months that made my participation in this project possible. They have shaped and formed much of the content I have contributed to this book. In my biased opinion, the people of First Baptist meet the criteria of the Future Faith Churches. They courageously live the balance of "soul care" and "social connectedness."

The team that I have worked with over the years at First critiqued my writing and my ideas. My colleague and friend at First Baptist, Brian Craig worked on the church model developed in Chapter 6. Greg, Dawn, Carol and Debby, thank you for the team ministry we share. Bev Bye, my secretary, spent extra time faxing, typing, and e-mailing the work I produced.

Two people screened my work. Ken Badley and Dan Coleman, both writers and scholars, taught me about writing and challenged me to clarify and make the content more relevant. My mentor and friend George Baxter set the model for clergy leadership that I think is crucial for the church of the future. My parents provided the atmosphere where I learned a love and hope for the church.

Don has been a valued friend for a long time and our relationship deepened after he invited me to write this book with him. We have argued, laughed, and challenged each other – and while we don't always agree, my respect for him has only grown deeper.

Finally, I am grateful to my wife Carla, who knows that my inner fear is that I might be discovered to be "the emperor with no clothes," yet she has always encouraged me to write because she believed that I had something to say. She is my best critic and most cherished friend. As a behind the scenes editor, no one could be more rigorous or challenging.

These people are my community. They have shaped my writing, stimulated my content, and are teaching me what the church can be.

Numerous books have been written about the church over the last years. Many of them provide helpful clues on how congregations might minister more effectively. Yet as Canadians we are still struggling with taking our own context and culture seriously. We believe *Future Faith Churches* is not just another book to be added to an already crowded library shelf. These are stories of real churches in real places, of people and congregations who are living both sides of the gospel equation. They inspired faith for the future in us. Our hope is they will inspire you too.

Gary Nelson

INTRODUCTION

A calculating young man had his eye on his next promotion. Ambition motivated him to take advantage of the fact that his boss was about to celebrate a birthday. He mused, "If I send a gift, that would give me an edge."

The young man's flair for style covered the reality that he was really a committed cheapskate. He went to an exclusive store that specialized in expensive china. When the attendant came to serve him, he politely asked, "Do you have any broken china? I'm looking for something that is very expensive, but already broken."

The attendant was confused. But, trained to be courteous, she replied, "Let me check to see what might be available."

When the attendant returned, she smiled graciously. "Luck is with you today," she explained. "We have a very expensive broken vase that has not yet been discarded."

With a broad grin, the young man negotiated a nominal price for a broken vase, which, in its original form, would have been an exquisite gift. Then he made a specific request.

"Please wrap up the broken vase in a very special gift-wrapped box, and send it to this man." He provided the name and address of his boss.

The attendant took the fragments of the vase away to the shipping department, to do their customary quality service.

The young man's strategy was flawless. His boss would receive a gift. He would open it, and find that the gift had been damaged in transit. The young man would get the credit, without the cost.

Later, the young man would call. When he learned that his gift had been damaged, he would express suitable regret. But obviously, he couldn't be held responsible for what had happened en route.

Calculating his odds, at the right time the young man called his boss. They had a contrived conversation. When the moment seemed right, the young man asked, "Did you receive my birthday gift?"

"Yes, I did," his boss replied. There was an awkward pause. Then his boss continued. "I was a bit confused, though. I'm still trying to figure out why all the pieces of the broken vase were all separately gift-wrapped."[1]

THE CRISIS IN OUR CHURCHES

That story – whether it is true or invented – seems to us to identify the problems of many churches today. The gospel is something like that expensive vase. It is valuable. It is costly – living it exacts a certain price. And it is currently broken. Fortunately, it has not yet been thrown out.

Many of today's churches resemble the ambitious young cheapskate. For a variety of reasons, historical and social, they have received a broken vase. Instead of embracing a faith that is full and complete, they have gift-wrapped separate pieces of the gospel, and offered those fragments to their congregations as if they were the whole counsel of God. In doing so, they diminish the beauty of a balanced and comprehensive gospel. Instead of a full-fledged faith, the people of God are left with compartmentalized faith. Essential segments of the gospel are isolated and deleted from the whole.

They have gift-wrapped separate pieces of the gospel, and offered those fragments to their congregations as if they were the whole counsel of God.

At the risk of caricaturing, some sectors of the Christian church are content to announce the gospel in words with little regard for the deeds of the faith they so passionately proclaim. Others are so captured by the need around them that they passionately serve hot meals and pour cups of cold water without ever acknowledging the name of Christ.

Similarly, some preachers eloquently present the eternal need for personal salvation, without ever linking new found faith with expectations for serving others. Other preachers lament injustices that scar God's creation and laud the merits of serving others, without any overt emphasis on helping people get more closely connected with Christ.

The consequences of both extremes are predictable. The Christian church is polarized; personal faith is separated from social concern. Regrettably, unless parishioners and members of congregations resist this fragmentation, they are left with less than God intended for them.

Tragically, the Great Commandment that Jesus left us, his summary of the wisdom of his historic faith, is fractured. "Love God with all your heart and soul and mind and strength," he said, "and love your neighbor as yourself." When churches gift-wrap fragments of the gospel, love for God is separated from love for neighbor; love for neighbor is disconnected from love for God.

This overemphasis of one-sided faith creates lopsided churches. Cultivation of an unbalanced faith produces splintered and incomplete people. A long-time advocate for a complete and balanced gospel, Ron Sider, asserts, "Most churches today are one-sided disasters. In some suburban churches, hundreds of people come to Jesus and praise God in brand new buildings, but they seldom learn that their new faith has anything to do with wrenching inner-city poverty just a few miles away. In other churches, the members write to their senators and lobby the mayor's office, but they understand little about the daily presence of the Holy Spirit. And they would be stunned if anyone asked them personally to invite their neighbors to accept Christ."[2]

Evangelical protagonist Jim Wallis shares the same view. "Churches today are tragically split between those who stress conversion but have forgotten its goal, and those who emphasize Christian social action but have forgotten the necessity for conversion."[3]

Discerning the dilemma, E. Stanley Jones once stated: "An individual gospel without a social gospel is a soul without a body, and a social gospel without an individual gospel is a body without a soul. One is a ghost, and the other is a corpse."

Ghosts and corpses were not God's original image of the church.

Fortunately, not all churches have fallen for the "broken vase" understanding of the gospel. The good news is that some churches – in every denomination and religious tradition – have found ways to embrace faith that is both personal and social. They consistently invite people whom they influence to experience personally the living Christ in their lives, as well as to respond compassionately and practically to people who have specific needs.

It would be simplistic to pretend that even in the most lop-sided churches the spheres of personal and social are totally isolated from each other. Total compartmentalization of personal faith from social concern is a theoretical notion. Even in the most "conversion-oriented" churches, there are people who go out and live their faith in food banks and political parties; even in the most "social justice" churches, there are people who study the Bible, join prayer groups, and passionately pursue a closer communion with their God. Any complete separation of "words of proclamation" from "deeds of compassion" is an artificial exercise.

Nevertheless, we believe that the thesis still stands. In the 20th century, organized religion in Canada has too often drawn a line between calling for personal faith in Jesus Christ, and focusing on a faith that calls the committed to pursue justice and do good deeds in Christ's name.

The purpose of this book is to cement together the importance of personal faith with the importance of social concern, of soul care with social care. We want to affirm the beauty of a balanced and undivided gospel. Our intent is to celebrate the integrity of a complete faith, the worth of a holistic gospel. Without being arrogant or judgmental, we contend that one-sided faith fails the test of Christian and biblical integrity.

Our main methodology is to tell some of the stories of 14 specific churches in Canada who are linking both sides of the faith – personal and social. These particular churches were selected from 285 churches that were nominated by a cross section of clergy representing various denominations and

Christian faith traditions. As well as being thriving and vital, the nomination criteria asked clergy to identify churches that had reputations for inviting their parishioners to experience personal faith in Christ while also being involved in social concern ministries. During the research process, we evaluated 418 survey responses from the 14 churches, and conducted carefully designed focus group sessions and interviews with the senior clergy from each church. The participating churches are identified in Appendix 1; other appendices define our methodology. It is our conviction that although the 14 churches identified are, in a variety of ways, far from perfect, they are "Future Faith" churches. They show us effective ways to "be the church" in the 21ˢᵗ century.

We also acknowledge that, in the equation of reality, combining their stories portrays the whole to be much more than the sum of their individual parts. But still, they are leading-edge churches for the 21ˢᵗ century. They deserve our attention. Our hope is that many other Christian faith communities across the nation will be inspired to join the journey toward Christian wholeness and biblical integrity too.

1

THE HERITAGE OF FUTURE
FAITH CHURCHES

If Canadians were not allowed to talk about the weather, considerable numbers of conversations would never get started.
Given the influence of massive oceans on both coasts, frigid
tundra winters in the north and the Great Lakes' induced tropi-
cal humidity in the summers, conversations across the nation
naturally begin with "weather talk." One thing we have in common as Canadians is the weather.

Another thing we have in common is the upheaval in our
value systems. It's hard enough to forecast the weather. No
one could have forecast how a devastating storm of rampaging secularism would damage the foundations of Christendom
in Canada. In the last century, the forces of secularism spread
havoc on the common assumptions that Canada was a Christian nation.

Historian John Webster Grant uses the metaphor of an
earthquake to describe the effect of secularism on the Canadian church:

*Like an earthquake that disarranges the topography of a region
and blocks outlets of its streams, the dramatic secularization of*

Canadian society interrupted the flow of Canadian church history and deflected some of its main thrusts from what had seemed to be their predetermined targets.[1]

Less dramatically, and over a much longer period of time, another series of spiritual storms would inflict damage on what had been a widespread consensus among Canada's Protestant churches. Eventually, the differences between liberal and conservative convictions in Canada's mainline and evangelical churches would drive a wedge between the people of God and split the church into two camps. Regrettably, Christian mainliners and Christian evangelicals would live in the same communities, neither relating to each other nor speaking the same religious language.

STARTING WITH AGREEMENT

At the beginning of this century, the nation's Protestants were united. With few exceptions, Canadians entered the current century on the confident footing of social consensus and shared mission.

Canada was unique. William Brackney discusses the uniqueness of the early North American Christian experience. He says that in Canada the vast frontier allowed countless religious associations to flourish so that "denominational understanding led to a toleration of each other's right to maintain one's religious position ... [so that] even the Old World faiths came to coexist with each other and understand that the Kingdom of God was broad and inclusive indeed."[2] Therefore, during the last decades of the nineteenth century and the first decade of this century, Canadian churches in English-speaking Canada were largely united in "the moral and spiritual crusades of evangelical Protestantism."[3] Sociologist

S.D. Clark suggests that there are few coun-
tries in the western world in which religion
exerted as great an influence on the development of the community as in Canada.[4]

In Quebec, the Catholic church was culturally dominant and politically influential.
The church had uncontested institutional and
social presence. Parish priests embodied pre-
eminent status and personal power. That too has changed,
as all can now recognize. In Roman Catholic circles, polarization also exists. On the one side, Catholic faithful are especially concerned about issues of personal morality, with
their focus on such matters as abortion, euthanasia, and
sexual lifestyle choices. On the other side, another segment
of the faithful give their attention to social justice issues:
women's rights, protection of the environment, systemic economic matters ... When the faithful gather for mass, different styles of worship within the Catholic tradition tend to
distinguish one orientation from the other.

The Catholic story is significant, but the intent of this chapter is to trace the turning points in the Protestant story that
eventually led to the mainline and evangelical polarization
that still exists today.

Historians agree that the major Protestant denominations
– Anglican, Methodist, Presbyterian and Baptist – were the
shaping institutions of English speaking Canada. Although
there were quarrels and rivalries, a shared vision of mission
resulted in interdenominational cooperation which gave
practical expression to the slogan of the new nation based on
ancient words of the psalmist, "He shall have dominion from
sea to sea." (Psalm 72:8) Accustomed to influence in the intellectual, social and cultural life of Canadians, the churches

**In Canada the
vast frontier
allowed
countless
religious
associations to
flourish.**

were unprepared to cope with accelerated change that pushed Canada into the forefront of modern nations between 1914 and 1945.[5]

The immigration wave that swept over the Canadian prairies in the early decades of this century injected evangelical energy back into the Canadian church scene. The smaller evangelical churches which had been the lesser lights in the Canadian church picture shone more brightly. Their biblical, more conservative and often anti-modernist approaches helped them weather the cultural storms and in time linked them with a broader Canadian public.

WWI, the depression, and WWII had a profound impact on Canadians and can be used to evaluate the place of the church in our society. Tracing those influences into the 1960s, when a cultural earthquake shook most pillars of our society and toppled many institutions, will help to frame the current picture of the modern Canadian church.

The shock waves of the 1960s shattered shared assumptions and replaced them with doubts and dissent. The tremors extended to public policy debates and supper table arguments. The loss of a Christian consensus generated haranguing at church business meetings and shaded barber shop and beauty salon gossip. By the early 1970s, although very few people perceived it yet, Christendom in Canada was dead.

While we should recognize the permanent change in our cultural topography, we should not undervalue the Christian heritage which was once so prominent on the cultural landscape. The historic foundations of our church institutions were based on the solid rock of social compassion and reinforced by the steel of evangelical conviction. Retracing the flow of church history into the '60s will help us understand what we surrendered, and why the '70s, '80s and '90s became decades of social fragmentation.

The primary threat to the church of the next century will come if we lay its foundations solely on the sandy mire of pluralistic secularism. The aspiration of this chapter is to affirm the virtues of our heritage that have the potential to redirect our energies for the 21st century.

1900-1920: A LEGACY FROM ANOTHER CENTURY

When Canada entered the 20th century, the Protestant church stood at the center of national life. The people of God were united in purpose, socially compassionate, and evangelically vibrant. They were the recipients of the rich legacy of 19th century faith which has been described as Canada's evangelical century.[6] Prior to WWI "there was little resistance in Protestant circles to the evangelical moralism" that the nation's churches rallied around.[7]

The Social Gospel was the centerpiece of this evangelical moralism. In the first years of this century this movement had animated many Canadian Christians to "bring all society as well as the individual into conformity with the teachings of Jesus Christ."[8] Influenced by British socialism and German theology, it was also injected with American optimism. The pervasive sense of progress throughout society added momentum to the Gospel-motivated message that believed in human perfectibility and the ability to break the "evils which attended growing secularization" through religious faith and moral strength.[9]

The Social Gospel of that time should not be confused with the form it took later in its life. It was not a protest movement, nor a form of political dissent. It was a vision, which believed that what the Bible calls "the Kingdom of

God" or "the new Jerusalem" could be created here on earth, in one form or another. As a vision, it was virtually taken for granted by all of Canada's churches.

1914: WORLD WAR I AND THE SOCIAL GOSPEL

The moral strength of Canada's Christian institutions was greatly tested by the Great War of 1914–1918. The same nations who considered themselves the epitome of Christian society employed "scientific butchery" in the first modern "total war." The millennium that most Social Gospellers had hoped for was lost in the carnage of new weaponry that included poison gas and aerial bombardments.

Canadian society, while not a battlefield, totally mobilized itself to fight on the side of the British Empire. Tens of thousands of young men who had triumphantly marched off to Europe singing glorious battle hymns were slaughtered.

Canadian Protestant churches were heavily implicated in sending young men to the European devastation. Parliament originally mobilized Canadian forces for a war that was to be short in duration – "the troops will be home by Christmas" was the promise. Because the Crown and the Cross were so connected, "to an extent that many churchmen later regretted, the pulpit became a center of recruitment."[10]

The churches' complicity in the wartime propaganda prompted many Canadians, including many veterans, to eventually write off the "practical failure of Christianity."[11] Social Gospel moralism was put on the defensive. The prevailing evangelical consensus began, for the first time, to give way to the forces of secularism. New biblical scholarship that questioned the literal interpretation of Scripture, other secularist pressures such as Darwinism, and the growth of comparative religion began to di-

vide the church into modernist and tradi-
tionalist camps.[12]

A clear example of the practical collapse
of the evangelical consensus was the end
of prohibition. During the 1914–1918 period every province had passed prohibition
legislation, largely at the request of Cana-

The lines of fissure can be clearly seen in the student movements of the 1920s.

dian social reformers from both evangelical and liberal
denominations. "But even before the War was over, the
consensus on this reform began to dissolve. The toll was
great. Not only was the reform lost but so too was the
coalition that had struggled for its implementation."[13]
Legislation was rescinded in all areas of Canada – except
PEI which held out until 1926 as Canada's only "dry"
province.

While there were many splinters, the majority of churches
began to move along a denominational divide. The more established, culturally dominant congregations began emphasizing the gospel task of *social* work. The smaller, and sometimes relatively new, church movements emphasized the gospel task of *soul* work. Although this may seem at first glance
like an inconsequential division, those representing progressive mainline congregations and those representing traditional evangelical churches were increasingly driven away
from their 19th century shared heritage. They began to edge
away from each other and to this day have never regained
their former level of consensus.

THE 1920s INSTITUTIONALIZING SEGMENTS OF SOCIETY

Fueled by prohibition's end, the Roaring Twenties symbolized Canadians' desire for a measure of self-indulgence. It
also marked the institutionalization of the post-war segmen-

tation in Canadian society. And these "new lines of fissure would only widen in succeeding years."[14]

The lines of fissure can be clearly seen in the student movements of the 1920s. Over 4000 veterans returned from the battlefields of Europe to university campuses across Canada. They came back radically changed by their experiences.

Many of these soldiers climbed out of their trenches, turned away from active religious involvement, and embraced the secularist ideas that were more prominent among their European allies. As Grant puts it, "Soldiers brought back to Canada memories not merely of Flanders mud and *mademoiselles* from Armentieres but of varied cultural patterns in many parts of the world."[15]

A second group of veterans who crawled out of the trenches and turned against the established church were soldiers who did not think the church was liberal enough. They embraced what they believed was a more reflective and responsive faith, a faith that was motivated by a justice-criticism and was ready to wrestle with the social issues of the day. Students at the University of Guelph, including many young veterans, launched the clearest expression of this movement during the Christmas break of 1920–21. They founded the Student Christian Movement (SCM). "Theologically," claims Robert Wright, "it was the most liberal organization in Canadian Protestantism in the 1920s celebrating scientific inquiry and humanizing Jesus unabashedly."[16]

A third group of veterans came back convinced that their churches were already too liberal. And so the same campuses that hosted SCM meetings began to host a competitor. The people involved were a self-consciously conservative fraternity deliberately distinct from the SCM movement. Originally rooted in Britain at Oxford and Cambridge, the

InterVarsity Christian Fellowship (IVCF) established student-led movements on Canadian campuses. In 1929, three groups representing the universities of Toronto, Manitoba and Western Ontario met to formally create the IVCF in Canada. Among the students attracted to this new fellowship were those who found the liberal posture of the SCM uncongenial. From the start the IVCF "fashioned itself as an evangelical alternative" on campuses across Canada.[17] These students were just as earnest as their SCM classmates in their desire to impact society. But they chose an evangelical-energizing strategy to motivate their mission.

1925: CHURCH UNION AND THE RISE OF EVANGELICAL CONGREGATIONS

At a denominational level, the founding of the United Church of Canada in 1925 offers a symbol and paradigm for the segmentation of Christian Canada.

In the Canadian west, particularly, two kinds of church growth were taking place. On the one hand, a number of small churches were discarding their traditional denominational ties and forming "Union" churches. Though their role is not often recognized or celebrated, they were a strong force pushing their mainline parents into church union. Either the Methodist, Presbyterian, and Congregational denominations would amalgamate into the United Church, reducing the number of different denominations in Canada, or these local "Union" churches would become effectively a new and additional denomination.

At the same time, also in the west, a decidedly fundamentalist flavored evangelical heritage was establishing institutional roots of its own.

John Webster Grant argues that church union was a product of "the spirit of consensus that had characterized liberal Protestantism in Canada in the first decade of the twentieth century."[18] The Social Gospel movement, though already breaking up as a national force by the time of union, was nonetheless a major motivating factor. The United Church of Canada inherited most of what was left of this movement as a last will and testament from the 19th century tradition of gospel-based social concern.

And a fitting recipient it was. The United Church became the nation's largest Protestant denomination, encompassing 20 per cent of the Canadian population.[19] Although the Presbyterian split over union cast a shadow over the celebration, the leaders of the new denomination embarked on making the United Church the nation's national church.

Unfortunately for Social Gospel purists, "the maintenance of large, pluralistic institutions requires tolerance and a willingness to balance the claims of divergent interests."[20] Not surprisingly, then, the United Church's desire to express a national vision meant the denomination would progressively emerge as the "most theologically open-minded denomination in Canada." From the closing of the June 10, 1925, ceremony of Church Union until today the United Church has been subject to charges of "doctrinal looseness and accommodation to secular society."[21] This looseness further watered down the Social Gospel evangelical heritage and, in the opinion of many, allowed the "Social" side of the equation to eclipse the "Gospel" side of the equation. In fact, according to John Stackhouse, "the general direction of the denomination throughout the century has been away from things that united evangelicals."[22]

In juxtaposition to the social focus of the massive new United Church with its modernist and inclusivist approach were the smaller and more fundamentalist denominations with their traditional and exclusivist approach. While still representing only a small percentage of Canadians, these churches experienced remarkable growth during the 1920s. Conservatives wanted to stop what they saw as the erosion of evangelical orthodoxy and, "in response to the inroad made by modernism in the early 20th century, the right wing of conservative evangelicalism in both Canada and the United States began to close ranks."[23] Thus began what might be called the "evangelical consensus."

With only a few exceptions, Canadians avoided the all-out fundamentalist-modernist wars of the American churches.

The war years and the 1920s were the heyday for some of the more well-known evangelical denominations. These church movements, often labeled sectarian, were not all new to Canada. Many had been part of the frontier experience since the 1800s. But with a huge influx of immigration early in the 20th century, these movements began to expand rapidly. For example, between 1911 and 1921 the Salvation Army grew by a remarkable 83 percent and by a respectable further 31 percent during the 1920s.[24]

Because the growth of many evangelical churches was partly the result of immigration, the style and character of those churches was largely shaped by the new immigrants. For example, in Alberta by 1911, 22 per cent of Albertans had come from the US; by 1920 it was estimated that up to 50 per cent of farmers in southern Alberta were of American origin.[25] As a result, Alberta church culture is often still cited as having similarities and linkages with its southern theological cousins: American, conservative, evangelical and leaning toward fundamentalism. Even though, as David Elliott noted, fundamentalist theology with its emphasis upon biblical literalism, a conversion experience and a separatist moral code "did not fit well into the Canadian religious ethos."[26]

A style of evangelical faith that was more compatible with Canadians drew support from Presbyterians, Anglicans, mainline or Federation Baptists and other smaller evangelical groups. This less fundamentalist form of evangelicalism was more engaged in the broader social debate, believed in the divine, if not literal, inspiration of Scripture and in personal holiness, but left the application of the latter up to the individual believer.[27] Christians of this persuasion were found in communities with longstanding British immigration, particularly southern Ontario and in BC's lower mainland.

With only a few exceptions, Canadians avoided the all-out fundamentalist-modernist wars of the American churches. During the '20s, there were Canadians concerned about the perceived cultural drift from traditional Christianity. But they responded in a less militant tone than evangelicals in America. According to John Stackhouse, the only communities in Canada to experience a "genuine fundamentalist-modernist schism" were the Baptists of Ontario and British Columbia.[28] The most famous confrontations between Baptists centered on McMaster Divinity College and the scathing attacks from self-confessed fundamentalist warrior T. T. Shields who charged the theological faculty at the institution with modernism, worldliness, and heresy. The echoes of that schism still linger in Baptist circles today.

Historians assess the Canadian way by suggesting that our "lingering ritualism and isolationism" shielded Canadians from strident dialogue.[29] Religious leaders followed the various theological debates "with characteristic moderation.

Outright 'modernist' denials of key orthodox doctrines, there-fore, were relatively rare in mainline Protestantism outside intellectual circles."[30]

Nevertheless, clear segments of Canadian religious life had begun to form: secularism, liberalism, and evangelicalism. John Webster Grant summarizes: "The changed atmosphere of the 1920s was a reflection in Canada of a process of secu-larization that had been affecting western civilization for cen-turies but was sped up by the first world war."[31] He contends that the liberal concerns of the SCM probably were an accu-rate representation of where Canadian society as a whole was moving. And while conservatism was on the rise in Canada, Grant concludes that church and culture were still at peace with each other. He writes, "Despite protests on the right and desertions on the left, their churches retained their cus-tomary place in the center of Canadian community life."[32]

1930s AND 1940 SOCIAL PRAGMATISM VS PERSONAL SPIRITUALITY

Out of the 1920s, mainline Protestant church leaders dragged the tattered remains of a church consensus into the decade of the Great Depression. The theological pretext of that consen-sus, the Social Gospel vision, was already exhausted from the challenges of the First World War. Its optimistic base was fur-ther trampled underfoot by the jobless men shuffling their way through the soup kitchen lines of the Depression. Outrage against the hardships and injustices of the Depression, and exploitation of human misery by the industrial "barons" of the period, fueled the most vigorous remnants of that Social Gospel heritage in the work of leaders like James Woodsworth.

World War II in 1939 finally put an unceremonious end to the wavering lilt of the Social Gospel's hopes and hymns.

The difficult circumstances of the times did not trigger a downturn in church attendance and religious activity. Just as post WWII generated a dramatic upswing in Canadians' standard of living, Protestant churches grew beyond the expectations of "all but the most sanguine prophets."[33] The growth, however, was based on neither the social concern moralism nor the gospel oriented evangelism of the past. As University of Manitoba's John Stackhouse ominously points out, "The growth did not necessarily indicate increased influence for the churches in Canadian society and culture ... For, to use a Canadian pun, while industries and churches can boom with success, so does lake and river ice as it begins to break up in the spring."[34]

THE 1930s: IN THE DEPRESSION
NEW RELEVANCE, NO RESOURCES

The Roaring Twenties' fashion for self-indulgence ended abruptly with the dawn of the Dirty Thirties. The Crash of 1929 and the ensuing economic decline came as a rude awakening for church leaders and the public alike.[35] The impact has been likened to a "fireball in the night to denizens of an allegedly fireproof building."[36]

At denominational headquarters across Canada, the situation was not unlike the current "Nasty Nineties." The watchword in the 1930s was "cuts." Office and college staffs were cut. Ministers' salaries were cut. Funding for missions was cut. But for many churches the overriding concern was for those Canadians most debilitated by the depression.[37] Consequently, operating deficits grew. Canadians who had been enjoying the new fruits of secularization in the 1920s discovered that the presence of the church meant more to them than they had realized. "One western layman told his home mission society, 'The bootleggers have gone, the movies have gone, credit is gone, social life is gone, but thank God the Church remains.'"[38]

Hindsight confirms that the 1930s was the last hurrah for the Social Gospel. The old style Social Gospel went political. Inspired by leaders with Christian convictions, the forerunner of today's New Democratic Party (NDP), the Co-operative Commonwealth Federation (CCF) won seats in the House of Commons and in 1944 became the ruling party in Saskatchewan. The CCF, influenced by proponents of the Social Gospel such as former Methodist minister James Woodsworth and Baptist Tommy Douglas, "sought a socialist alternative to capitalism, at least in part out of a desire to Christianize the social order."[39]

The politicization of the Social Gospel took place primarily in mainline parishes. Accordingly, mainline churches moved more and more into social welfare, driven by secular notions of economic justice.

At the same time, evangelical and fundamentalist churches remained faithful to their "soul work" calling and responded to the Depression differently. Evangelicals interpreted the desperate economic times as an opportunity to respond to hurting people's search for religious meaning. Even though restrained by fiscal austerity, the popularity of Canadian fundamentalists and conservative evangelicals steadily increased. They capitalized on the considerable rise in interest of "old time religion." In doing so, however, evangelicals continued to distance themselves from their social gospel roots.

CLEARING UP POTENTIAL MISUNDERSTANDINGS
A question worth asking is, Why did Canadian evangelicals so decidedly emphasize personal conversion over social compas-

sion? After all, Canadian evangelicals had been united with other denominations over issues of social concern in the late 1900s and early twentieth century. The coalition around prohibition that broke down after WWI was one such example. Evangelicals had also been involved in social issues ranging from Sunday closings to child labor laws.

As a voice for current evangelicals, John Stackhouse warns Canadian readers of church history not to be led astray by the American version of history. Stackhouse resists the assumption that Canadian evangelicals abandoned their social ministry in reaction to the mainline embrace of social activism. Instead, he proposes that evangelical church leaders "blithely left the driving of the social 'bus' to government – at least until the 1960s when there could be no more illusion of a Christian consensus in Canadian life."

David Moberg, in his analysis of the evangelical church, contends that a caricature of the mean-spirited evangelical unconcerned with the plight of his or her neighbors is unfaithful to evangelical social heritage. Rather, he suggests, they continued to approach these social concerns from a position of evangelical orthodoxy. Consistent with their understanding of how God works in people, evangelicals looked at social problems believing that personal conversion to Jesus Christ would change the individual. The power of conversion would turn a dishonest man into an honest citizen, a criminal would become law-abiding, and a mentally-ill person would be healed. Moberg concludes that since many evangelicals "believe all social problems are at root merely personal problems, evangelistic Christians think that solving personal problems through converting souls to Jesus Christ will resolve the problems of the world."[40]

While it is inaccurate to suggest Canadian evangelicals were unconcerned about the social welfare of their neighbors, it is equally mistaken to assume mainline Christian social activism doesn't have a worthy spiritual motivation. Again, Moberg offers clarity by observing that for socially involved Christians, "doing good for them is the highest form of preaching, for they all see it as conveying the message of God's love to all mankind by deeds and examples. Therefore, they insist that the battle against sin must be waged against inequities and injustices in the social order that twist the personal lives of individuals and do violence to their high status as creatures made in the image of God."[41]

The end of WWII marked the end of liberal idealism.

The 1930s encouraged Christians to put their faith into action. They were tough times on the Canadian landscape. Christians could not stand by unconcerned. Mainly in the crucible of the prairie dustbowl, evangelicals preached and practiced what they keep doing today. They sought to help society by redeeming sinful people with the light of the gospel. At the same time, mainline churches established their practice of helping individuals by illuminating societal sin with the same sacred gospel light. In that crucial era, organizational lines were drawn that continued to polarize evangelical and mainline Christians from each other. Sunday morning sermons focused on different parts of the same Bible and separate Christian cultures were cultivated.

THE 1940s THE IMPACT OF WWII
For conservative evangelicals and fundamentalists, the Declaration of War in September 1939 confirmed "beyond any doubt the error of liberal modernism and its absurd notions of evolution and human perfectibility." Liberals were hard

pressed to refute this conclusion and in many liberal circles there was a move back to orthodoxy. Says Wright: "Man's inability to remedy the Depression, thwart an Adolf Hitler, or prevent a second global war marred the idea of human progress and confirmed the hard reality of human sin."[42]

Reinhold Niebuhr, the American theologian who influenced many Canadian church leaders, attacked the naïveté of liberal Protestantism.[43] He believed that the Kingdom of God on earth was an unattainable ideal, prevented from full fruition because of man's sinfulness. Justice could not be attained by moral appeal, but only by brokering an equilibrium of power between society's competing interests. "In light of this, the Christian was to work for social improvement, yet without any illusion that it would eventually lead to perfection."[44]

Whether spoken from a Pentecostal pulpit or an Anglican lectern, the circumstances of the 1940s made the need for divine intervention seem self-evident, and the recognition of original sin brought a sense of relief in the way it placed humans in the context of tragic world events.[45]

The end of WWII marked the end of liberal idealism. By 1945 "the once-powerful idea of building the Kingdom of God on earth was dead."[46] The social reform torch was passed from liberal church society to secular segments of society, most notably the CCF's successor, the New Democratic Party. The mainline or liberal churches still believed in social awareness, but gave up the triumphal pursuit of building God's Kingdom in Canada. It was a time of reflection but not re-crimination for the proponents of the Social Gospel.

John Webster Grant describes the post 1945 mood: "In contrast with the United States, where the reaction against theological liberalism proved divisive in many denominations, the general mood on Canada was one of sober reappraisal. Wild charges of communism against respected church leaders that abounded in the United States during the ascendancy of Joseph McCarthy were seldom echoed in Canada."[47]

1945 NEED FOR NORMALCY

After 1945, the forces of communism, the scientific method, automation, global industrialization, and secularism put the church in most of the world on the defensive. Kenneth Scott Latourette considers these forces, then concludes, "It appeared ominous for the future of Christianity that the forces that were menacing Christianity had their rise in Christendom. ... They would seem, accordingly, to be more destructive of Christianity than of the other religions of mankind."[48]

Although post-war relief was everywhere, thoughtful Christians could not deny that so much of the destruction of the troubled first half of the 20th century was spawned by nations and peoples professing faith in the Christian God of love and compassion. Latourette sums up the state of affairs: "... The 1930s were followed by a holocaust which proved to be even more widespread and devastating than the stage which had its inception in 1914. While this, too, subsided in 1945, in the early 1950s mankind viewed the future with fearful apprehension, wondering whether worse was still not to come."[49]

That "worse" was quickly symbolized by the mushroom cloud of nuclear explosion.

The consequences of the times meant that "even in western Europe ... churchgoing was coming to be regarded as a harmless eccentricity."[50] But in things religious, Canada and the United States stood apart. As Grant notes "What happened in Canada, as in North America generally, was so different that it remains to this day a source of wonder. Soon after 1945 until about 1960 there was a general boom in all things religious."[51]

But boom didn't necessarily mean better. Stackhouse warns, "It seems there was less of a revival of genuine and lasting spirituality in the post-war boom than of a revival of general cultural conservatism and consumerism of which church involvement was a component." In fact, Stackhouse says, when the 1960s and '70s hit with an assortment of social earthquakes and aftershocks, churches collapsed precisely because of the shallow nature of religion in the 1950s.

THE 1950s CONSUMER BOOM VS SPIRITUAL VITALITY

Churchgoers in the 1950s wanted solid answers to many of the questions raised by the past two decades of warfare and poverty. But they were also faced with handling issues that unprecedented affluence delivered to them.[52]

Canadian soldiers left behind a wrecked and exhausted Europe and boarded ships bound for their dynamic and prosperous homeland. The economic energy that had gone into Canadian war efforts switched over to the peacetime production of consumer goods. The war had also brought about innovation in social welfare including unemployment insurance and family allowances.

The post-war approach to church attendance was mixed with the prevalent consumer values of the time. Post-war Canadians were eager for services of the church, but selective in which services they chose. While going to church was a uniquely North American thing to do, Canadians joined with other Western nations in viewing church involvement as being a part of leisure-time activities.[53] Sunday morning was mandatory, but Ed Sullivan ruled on Sunday night – unless one belonged to a conservative evangelical church.

Whether the religious flavor was Norman Vincent Peale or Billy Graham, the spirit of the '50s invited initiative and applauded opportunity.

The post-war approach to church attendance was mixed with the prevalent consumer values of the time.

John Webster Grant's analysis of Canadian church history sums up the impact of consumerism on church life. He writes, "Newly active members sought a product called religion in buildings that resembled attractive retail outlets. They went to church not so much to express conviction as to seek answers to questions, solutions to problems, and guidance in decisions… Suburbanites found it natural to choose denominations, as they chose banks or grocery chains, for their convenience of location or range of facilities."[54]

The phenomenal church growth of "the Fifties" was in a large part a result of demographics. The post-war boomers were having children; the Canadian population was soaring. Grant notes too, with clear-eyed realism, that the religious boom was also linked to "suburbia, where families with small children were most heavily concentrated and where the effects of increased affluence were most widely felt. The church merely inched ahead in small towns of static population, was unable to arrest decline in the inner city, and lost ground rapidly in rural areas."[55]

The splintering of church consensus that had taken place in previous decades was, ironically, exacerbated by the church growth of the 1950s. The boom in numbers and resources failed to encourage closer cooperation between denominations. Suburban expansion offered opportunities to erect new church buildings with larger sanctuaries, classrooms, dining halls and gymnasiums. In a 20 year period after the war, the United Church of Canada built 1500 new churches or halls and 600 new manses – averaging more than two every week![56] When church buildings could be filled and paid for with unprecedented ease, there was more competition for desirable building sights than cooperation over broader issues.[57]

Patterns of moral behavior also changed with the times. Eager to surround themselves with the amenities of life after 16 years of economic depression and global warfare, middle class Canadians "condemned earlier standards not as unrealistically high but as restrictive of natural human freedoms."[58] Accordingly, the traditional emphasis of some churches was moderated. The United Church, with its Methodist roots, had always supported voluntary abstinence from alcohol. But in the 1950s social drinking became accepted. Alcoholics Anonymous held meetings in church buildings.[59] Once again for the United Church and denominations which followed similar patterns, there was a loss of distinctiveness and an accommodation to secular norms.

PROBLEMS OF PROSPERITY

Affluence gave the churches a radical new challenge. Instead of their social consciences championing the plight of the deprived in society, mainline congregations overflowed with congregants enjoying unfamiliar prosperity. The new churches were filling up with people who suffered no obvious disadvantages, but who expressed great dissatisfaction and difficulty personally and in relationships. John Webster Grant observes, "Whether affluence intensified personal problems or merely provided more leisure for trying to solve them, churches found themselves drawn into the field of mental health."[60]

One of the issues, according to John Stackhouse, was that WWII veterans were unprepared for the return to civilian life, no matter how prosperous its promises. He comments, "Moral decline threatened as many soldiers left behind wartime lovers and self-indulgent recreational habits, returning home to strained or broken marriages and children they had not seen in years."[61] Certainly this would help explain Grant's observation that "the postwar malaise in personal relations was nowhere more evident than within the family circle." Therefore, during the demobilization years, marital problems were responsible for much of the demand for pastoral counseling in churches.[62]

The increasing demands of a counseling ministry tended to preclude a commitment to outreach and mission. Rather, they drew the mainline congregations into close league with the 20th century secular science of psychology. The social concern axis shifted from the familiar ground of economic justice to the less known issues of relational justice and the self-actualization of individuals. The consumer-mindedness of the time and the desire of many church leaders to be socially responsive took many denominations into uncharted territory in terms of theology and ministry.

RISE OF EVANGELICALISM

Christians who held to a "high" view of the inspiration and authority of the Scriptures, the importance of personal conversion, and the centrality of evangelism in the mission of the church, felt more and more estranged from the mainstream of many denominations.[63] These individuals, though still representing only a minority of Canadian Protestants, began to see themselves as part of a transdenominational fellowship that they would come to identify as "evangelical."[64]

Evangelical denominations had in fact, experienced rapid growth after 1945. They came to the prosperous 1950s with a concern for evangelism and salvation rather than social awareness and therapeutic ministry. Included in the evangelical movement are charismatic and non-charismatic churches such as the Salvation Army, Pentecostal Assemblies, Free Methodists, Baptists, Associated Gospel, Christian and Missionary Alliance, Mennonite Brethren, and the Church of the Nazarene.

The 1950s Protestant para-church movement primarily generated in the United States also injected energy and vision into the Canadian evangelical scene. Youth for Christ came across the border and hosted evangelistic Saturday night rallies for young people. Billy Graham emerged confidently proclaiming "the Bible says" and calling people of all ages to make decisions for Christ. In this same period, evangelist Bob Pierce pushed out the boundaries of the normal evangelical agenda and founded World Vision. While taking his gospel message to war-torn Korea, Pierce was overwhelmed by orphaned children roaming the streets. He went back to his room and wrote the words in the fly-leaf of his Bible that were to become his life's theme: "Let my heart be broken by the things that break the heart of God."[65]

Evangelicals now extended to every part of the country and increasingly attracted middle-class urbanites. Their main goal was to preach the gospel more effectively and to provide fuller opportunities for Christian experience.[66] They were not always charitable toward their mainline opposition. Evangelical denominations accused more conventional churches not of heresy but of spiritual deadness.[67] The mainliners had become so socially relevant, charged the evangelicals, that they had lost the soul-care side of Christian faith.

Unlike their mainline cousins, evangelicals did not compromise with the changing morals of the suburban sophisticates. And they certainly did not accept growth into the Christian life as a substitute for conscious conversion, nor social involvement as a sign of Christian witness. Rather they insisted on confronting every individual directly with the necessity of making a choice about Christ.[68]

The rules of life were being rewritten and they were not being rewritten according to Christendom.

The sometimes confrontational and always clear-cut message of evangelical groups was based on confidence in the reliability of the Bible. It was a very distinct and well-suited message for the times. Evangelicals were able to "to commend their product with complete sincerity, while their preference for direct methods of evangelism enabled them to take advantage of current techniques of salesmanship without embarrassment."[69] While some would critique evangelicals for their lack of compassion and question whether their methods were culturally Canadian, no one would doubt their conviction and desire to win people to the cause of Christ.

1960s SOCIAL PROTEST VS COMFORTABLE PEWS

The sixth decade of the second millennium provoked fundamental social shifts that restructured our society and our community values in revolutionary ways. In historian Sydney Ahlstrom's terms, the '60s were a time when "presuppositions that had held firm for centuries – even millennia – were being widely questioned. Some sensational manifestations came and went (as fads and fashions will), but the existence of a basic shift of mood rooted in deep social and institutional dislocations was anything but ephemeral."[70] Or more simply put, "New cosmic signs *were* being read in the sixties."[71]

Continuing to bask in the numerical growth of the '50s, "the Canadian pew was still comfortable" but the church was caught off guard.[72] The social turmoil of the decade dealt a knockout punch that left the church sprawled on society's canvas.

The decade was especially distressing for mainline and Catholic churches and their leaders. The shift from being cultural heavyweights used to landing solid punches rather than being dazed by opponents' blows was traumatic.

Evangelicals did not escape from being bruised by the blows inflicted by the decade either. Whatever one's church involvement, it was clear that the rules of life were being rewritten and they were not being rewritten according to Christendom. The Canadian populace was the referee, and the arms of secularism were being raised in victory.

A DEEPENING THEOLOGICAL DIVIDE

The cultural earthquake in the '60s and the lines of fissure which John Webster Grant warned about solidified into two great gulfs. The cultural gulf between church and society, and the theological gulf between the mainline and evangelical churches, grew wider.

Evangelicals in the '60s pretty much stuck with their ecclesiological knitting. Their inclination to construct closed theological systems and to keep focused on the Bible's teachings protected them from both the onslaughts of society and the temptations of trendy deviation. They continued to preach the good news of the need for Christ's forgiveness, attempt to motivate clear Christian witness, and create communities of faith that served the needs of their members.

The mainline church story was quite different. Compared to evangelicals, their more liberal and inclusive theological systems invited an embrace of the spirit of the age. While many clergy remained thoroughly orthodox, diverse thinkers either proclaimed the "death of God," insisted on an entirely "secular" interpretation of the gospel, or thoroughly "demythologized" the biblical message. Popularized by the force of mass media in combination with a wide range of writers, both clerics and lay people from all faith communities, opened up "a massive credibility gap in matters of faith and religion."[73] The emergence of liberation theology and the need to address the systemic causes of evil added fuel to the burning theological fires. The decade's radical movement in theology caused "a major reappraisal of the most assured grounds of the historic Judeo-Christian consensus."[74]

By the end of the '60s, mainline and evangelical churches lived in the same country, but they were neither relating to each other nor speaking the same religious language. Mainliners were focused on ecumenical concerns. Evangelicals were setting up their own ministerial associations. The gospel edge for mainline churches was sharpened with social concerns. The gospel edge for evangelicals was sharpened by the mission of rescuing souls. Instead of realizing their common enemy in rampaging secularization, mainline Christians and evangelical Christians were trapped in the tragic divisiveness of distrusting and judging each other.

When there is polarization that divides and conviction that controls, Larry Christenson offers insight and a timely reminder: "Both evangelical and social activists operate within the same mentality: within a theological box, a closed system of ready made answers, with little understanding or regard for other points of view." Evangelicals have their set of texts, centering on personal experience of salvation and a life of holiness. Social activists and mainliners both have their set of texts that emphasize the human side of social responsibility.[75]

CHURCH AND SOCIETY PART COMPANY
By the later '60s, declining growth rates and shrinking church budgets clearly signaled a widespread "loss of institutional vitality."[76] As John Stackhouse aptly expressed, "statistical fingers began to write on the ecclesiastical wall."[77] Evangelicals may have begun to attract a statistically significant number of people, compared to the mainline churches, but they did so in a society where the vast majority were turning away from *all* churches. The main statistic suggesting the peril of the mainline churches was the tendency of members of smaller evangelical denominations to attend church more regularly than those of larger ones.[78]

Coping with statistical signals, and realizing what you stand for is losing cultural significance, are two radically different matters. The 1960s' social protest was clearly a secular movement with secular aims. The aims of Christ were seldom seen as placard slogans for those in protest marches. The power of peace and the call to love became a signature of alternative subcultures rather than the rallying cry of Christians. In an age of political assassinations, nightmares about nuclear annihilation and the waking reality of napalm scorched bodies, the church lost its prophetic voice. For the first time since the founding of Canada, the church lost its moral authority.

Commentary on the social complexity of the '60s has produced thousands of books and many movies and television programs. Becoming overly simplistic has inherent dangers, but if there was one dimension of the '60s that profoundly affected the church it was that people took back for themselves the authority they had once granted to God and the church. By the end of the decade, for the majority, the right of personal conscience overruled dogma and doctrine. Obedience to God and directives from the church were replaced with the discretion of individual prerogative. Whether the issue related to sexuality, birth control, the role of women, or whether or not one should attend Sunday worship, personal choice preempted conformity. The veto vote was vested in the power of the person.

The aims of Christ were seldom seen as placard slogans for those in protest marches.

Broadly described, this change was away from an ethic of obligation to others and toward an obligation to self.[79] Although Canadians continued to use the church for rites of passage and occasional contact with the sacred, the will and ways of secularism replaced the will and ways of God and the church.

Once dominant at the center of national life, the churches – all churches – had been moved to the periphery. Seeking to pick up those who were having trouble floating in a sea of prosperous secularism, the Christian churches were little distinct from the other ships of faith afloat in the nation. Other ships were often buoyed by fad-based flings with Eastern religions, or lashed together as homemade rafts in opposition to the dominant culture. Yet these alternatives often attracted more Canadians aboard during the stormy 1960s than the once dominant Christian churches.

In a majority sense, Canadians turned their backs on all churches whether their emphasis was social or soul. By the end of the watershed decade of the '60s, Canadian Christendom was dead.

1970s TO 1990s: CHURCH GROWTH
VS SOCIAL TRANSFORMATION

As the nation turned the corner into the '70s, the Grand Canyon chasm between the church and secular society was self-evident. The call of the church to heed the truth of faith was no match for the demands of science to provide rational test-tube truth. Mainline and evangelical churches also found themselves on opposite sides of a wide and deep gorged river without any bridges to travel toward each other.

Evangelicals affirmed the importance of soul care while mainliners preached about the importance of social care. Instead of learning from each other's strengths, their separation meant both sides were content with propagating an incomplete and lopsided gospel.

Sociologist Reginald Bibby has carefully documented the state of religious affairs for both evangelical and mainline churches for this period of time. His benchmark setting and best selling book *Fragmented Gods* revealed the majority of Canadians as people with spiritual interest but lacking spiritual commitment. They are satisfied with "Religion à la Carte" and the availability of churches for rites of passage and celebrating the historical Christian holidays of Christmas and Easter.[80] Bibby's sequel, *Unknown Gods* statistically projects a dramatic slide downward for mainline churches and steady but modest gains for evangelical churches.

The '70s to '90s were not kind to mainline churches. As the dominant Protestant presence in the nation, mainline churches were used to building churches, hiring clergy, running programs, and welcoming Canadians into their programs. If you lived in the parish it was expected that you would be a part of the parish church. Mainline clergy had a long history of serving like chaplains to the community. If a prayer was needed to bring a touch of the sacred to a public occasion, they would appear with their visible clergy collars and express appropriate prayers in an orderly fashion. Their mainline history prepared them for maintaining the traditional, but it did not equip them to be mission driven in a secularized culture. Certainly those parishioners who continued to be involved celebrated the sacraments and received pastoral care. And leaders were far from passive. Decades of evangelism were announced; new ministry initiatives were explored. But more energy was invested in saving the church than either saving or serving the world.

In contrast, the evangelical church's history as religious underdogs, coupled with the mission driven nature of their understanding of ministry, positioned them to advance in the '70s and '80s. From their beginnings in Canada, evangelicals always had to try harder and to work with a competitive spirit. They were used to their minority status in the culture and unapologetically invited people to come to Christ and enter their folds. Evangelicals also found themselves in touch with an unstated but widespread cultural hunger. The human spirit refused to be downsized to test tubes and the limits of rational-only reality. The evangelical message to personally experience the forgiveness of Christ and the power of the Holy Spirit tapped into the hunger of the age. Responding to streams of United States strategies and conferences championing church growth, evangelicals reached out to win the world. By 1990, it is estimated that on a normal Sunday morning in Canada, there were more people worshiping in evangelical churches than there were in the combined total of the nation's mainline churches.

CONCLUSION

There is strong biblical support for the claim that the essence of the Christian gospel involves both personal faith and active social concern. The mission of the church, therefore, mandates *both* soul care and social care. One cannot help but wonder about the nature of the recent evangelical church growth when it is tested against the essence of the biblical gospel. What is happening spiritually to people when there is impressive church growth but little evidence of compassionate ministries or social transformation?

In the spirit of the Great Command, committed Christians are invited to be "love God and love your neighbor" people. In both Testaments, the Bible speaks on the subject frequently and clearly. (See sample next page.)

Since the third decade of the 20th century, Canadian churches and their leaders have leaned toward either soul care or social care. Instead of embracing both sides of the gospel equation, they have given allegiance to one without full regard for the other. As we turn the corner and head into the 21st century, Canadian Christians and their leaders have the opportunity to begin again. Just as the people of God did almost 100 years ago, we can be anchored on both the solid rock of evangelical conviction and social compassion. We can experience God's love as we inform our social consciences and express our love for people.

As we pursue God's hope that we be fully Christian, we can also learn from the Future Faith churches that are already pursuing the practice of both sides of the gospel equation.

Primary congregational focus	Old Testament	New Testament
Soul Care/ Personal Faith	Ezekiel 11:19-20 I will give them one heart, and put a new spirit within them; I will remove the heart of stone from their flesh and give them a heart of flesh, so that they may follow my statutes and keep my ordinances and obey them. Then they shall be my people, and I will be their God.	John 3:16 For God so loved the world that he gave his only Son, so that everyone who believes in him may not perish but may have eternal life.
Social Care/ Active Social Concern	Micah 6:8 What does the LORD require of you but to do justice, and to love kindness, and to walk humbly with your God?	Matthew 23:23 Woe to you, scribes and Pharisees, hypocrites! For you tithe mint, dill, and cummin, and have neglected the weightier matters of the law: justice and mercy and faith. It is these you ought to have practiced without neglecting the others.
Great Command: Soul Care & Social Care	Deuteronomy 6:5 & Leviticus 19:18 You shall love the LORD your God with all your heart, and with all your soul, and with all your might … and you shall love your neighbor as yourself: I am the LORD.	Matthew 22:36-40 "Teacher, which commandment in the law is the greatest?" He said to him, "'You shall love the Lord your God with all your heart, and with all your soul, and with all your mind.' This is the greatest and first commandment. And a second is like it: 'You shall love your neighbor as yourself.' On these two commandments hang all the law and the prophets."

2

DISCERNING THE SOUL OF FUTURE FAITH CHURCHES

Some people fear that there are dangers in letting real people in real churches tell their stories. Will they get it right? Will their experiences instill confidence in the claims of the gospel? Or will they stain the sacred with too much humanity and not enough God? Preacher and teacher William Willimon offers solid counsel when he says "We do well to stick to the church as we have experienced it rather than setting up some ideal picture of human community ... We are humans, and our communities invariably reflect our humanity at its best and at its worst."[1]

As we move attention from the historical state of the Canadian church to current reality, our intent is to let people speak out of their own experiences of faith and life in their churches. The numerous focus group participants with whom we talked in the course of gathering research for this book now have the chance to speak. Out of their messages we will discern the soul of Future Faith churches.

The focus group participants were identified by the churches where they worship. The individual churches which are the focus of this book – mainline, evangelical, Catholic, Aboriginal Pentecostal, and charismatic – are faith communities with enough similar stories to give them shared reputations. They were nominated and selected for study because they invite their parishioners to place their faith in the gospel and the person of Jesus Christ while at the same time motivating their people to express social compassion. They are "love God" and "love your neighbor" churches. Although surprises surfaced, when focus group participants and the clergy shared their personal experiences, certain themes emerged.

One of the core themes that repeatedly came out of the focus group sessions affirmed faith that is personal.

INTERVIEWER: "How are you different because of the influence of this church? How have you changed?"

RESPONSE: "What do I say? I think it is that now I have a relationship with God which I could not have said seven years ago. Or at least I'm developing a relationship. And I can say that out loud too. But I couldn't have seven years ago."

Future Faith churches affirm the conviction that being a Christian involves living in a relationship with God. The language is not always the same; there are different understandings about how people get started with God. But one way or another the Christian experience of God takes place at a very personal level.

Another common denominator is that Future Faith churches are consistently involved in compassionate ministries.

One exciting – and fairly typical – story of Future Faith churches was told to us by a pastor who worked as a volunteer high school chaplain. He had invested a lot of his time working with the counselors at a local school where he got to know the needs of young people in his community. This experience helped him understand how his church could respond to the needs of young people in a realistic and relevant way.

One way or another the Christian experience of God takes place at a very personal level.

After ten years of serving as a volunteer chaplain alongside high school counselors, the pastor was able to relate to young people suffering from trauma, particularly grief or family breakdown. In one instance, he was helping a young person who because of abuse had nowhere to live. Finding a home for the teen helped him bridge the strength of the church community with the needs of the wider community. Eventually the church developed "Lighthouse For Teens," a ministry for teenage girls.

The pastor recalls, "In a Sunday morning sermon I painted a picture of what four or five girls were going through in the school where I was chaplain. At the end of the sermon I simply said, 'Those of you who feel that you want to search this out and talk to me, we're going to meet on Tuesday night.' Seven people came. And those seven people met for two years around that issue: almost every month praying and researching how we could best meet the needs of those kids."

After a lot of study, the Lighthouse was set up. It was a place for kids who couldn't live at home. Set up like a home, with a resident adult, it was a safe environment. The Lighthouse carefully coordinated their ministry in conjunction with various community social agencies.

This activist pastor admitted that there are "rocky times" in a ministry like this. But he concluded with satisfaction that the lives of young teenagers were built up as was the church in the community. "We put 15 girls through the Lighthouse. I believe the Lighthouse really rescued those kids," he said. Then he added, "The group of seven felt a call to that ministry. They stuck with the ministry and they covenanted together to see it through. It became a small group. A cell group around a mission. That was one adventure."

These adventures are being undertaken by Future Faith churches in communities all across Canada. Following the focus group session and leadership interview in Kelowna, research assistant Daryl Thomson talked with me [Don] on the telephone. Recounting the dynamics of the previous day, he asked, "How is it possible that I can hear many of the same things from people in a Vineyard Church in British Columbia that you heard from Catholics in Ottawa? There are differences, but the similarities are staggering."

What accounts for so much commonality across different denominations and faith traditions that are structurally and functionally separated from each other? Part of the answer lies in "discerning the soul" of the 14 participating Future Faith churches.

Communities of Grace

Churches are not all the same. For example, many churches across the country are cloned by denominational determinism. Organizational traditions set the standard for the shape of the buildings, control the style of worship and frame ministry agendas. Other churches think of themselves as truth churches; they see themselves as Bible centered and doctrinally straight, and tend to believe that they have the final word on God's revelations. Some faith communities are knit together by liturgy and rituals. In more independent churches, the minister is the glue. The pastor in charge is the vision, the spokesperson, the orchestra leader, the authority, and the voice of God who holds it all together.

But whatever the denominational details, or lack thereof, Future Faith churches are communities of grace. They are laced with compassion and infused with mercy. Whether their denominational associations are conservative or more liberal, whether they are older parishes or younger congregations, grace abounds.

GRACED WITH ACCEPTANCE

Grace with acceptance is woven into the fabric of Future Faith churches. Like the artistic worship murals and banners that bring color and imagery to church sanctuaries, these churches are permeated with the beauty of an accepting grace. One Anglican focus group participant stated, "There is a non-judgmental tone here. For instance, everyone is invited to have communion ... You come, you get accepted, just as you are."

The grace of acceptance helped one United Church congregant develop a sense of "forgiveness for myself and acceptance of other people." Thinking about the consequences, he concludes, "My faith is taking root here." Similarly, a participant in a Vineyard church tells how people feel welcome in the church, "There's not a whole lot of phony Christianity where you have to hide who you are and be somebody you're not." A Chinese Baptist church attender is similar to the United and Vineyard churchgoers: "We don't want to look at people on the outside ... We are simply trying to help people live as Christians and follow what Christ has taught us."

These churchgoers believe that the acceptance exhibited in their faith communities is crucial. Another Baptist focus group participant says, "I would be really disappointed if this church lost its openness and acceptance. One of the things that really appeals to me is that you don't have to be perfect in order to be involved in something."

The church as a body of believers benefits when grace is extended without reservation. As a Christian Reformed participant explained, "We have members in our church who have been alcoholics. They've shown us a picture of what that's like. We have people who have gone into jail and come back out, and they've given us a picture of that. I don't know how many other churches have the opportunity to see how these people approach their Christianity."

Extending open arms to people is part of the spirit of Future Faith churches. They are inviting, accepting and certainly not judgmental. As a Catholic attender sums up, "People come first. It's love before law."

GRACED WITH COMPASSION

If acceptance has a twin sister, it is compassion. When compassion is present, mean-spiritedness is absent. Instead of nurturing harshness, vindictiveness, or the urge to censor, compassion leans sympathetically toward others. The inclination is to understand the other person's situation. Compassion is like love. It is not arrogant, rude, or intolerant. Compassion extends beyond self-interest. It offers the benefit of the doubt. In relationships, it is prepared to travel the second mile.

The souls of Future Faith churches are cradled in compassion. Assessing what happens in her church, one woman parishioner stated that "we accept the reality that the world is a very broken place and we're all broken people." Reflecting a general

spirit in Future Faith churches, a man commented: "We're often told we're on a journey.
Rather than you're in or you're out, everybody's
included."

**When
compassion
is present,
mean-
spiritedness
is absent.**

Speaking carefully, another person stated:
"I don't know exactly how to say this, but we were
probably the first church in our area to accept a
lady minister. We were the first church to accept a severely handi-
capped man as an assistant minister. We have people around
here that other churches didn't seem to welcome."

Other comments convey a similar spirit: "If somebody makes
a mistake, it's not, 'Well, you better leave the church now.'
Rather it's 'If you've made a mistake, we're not going to say
that this is okay, or this is not okay.' If the person is sorry,
'We're going to be with you. We're not going to abandon you.'"

Compassionate people know when it is important to stay
close, but they also know when to give distance. As one person explained, "One thing that helps draw people is the love
people have in the church for each other. It's not overbear-
ing, but people feel cared about without being smothered."

Columnist and broadcaster Tom Harpur writes that we all
walk with a limp. Our woundedness is an essential part of
our humanity, he asserts. Harpur is tuned into the Future Faith
wavelength. He explains that freedom to face failure is an
important part of community because it allows us to all live
at the same level. "There are no wholly strong, perfect human beings," he writes. "There are only the weak and those
who pretend not to be."[2]

GRACED WITH DIVINE ENERGY

If acceptance and compassion were the only virtues cradled in
the souls of Future Faith churches, they would be soothing to

the human spirit but they would lack spiritual energy and firm conviction. There is more to the story. In one focus group a participant blurted out, "This church is vibrant and full of energy." Another person enthusiastically expressed his feelings, "I like to tell people that our church is a fun and exciting place to be. It's got a dynamic ministerial team and that they should come and try it – come and experience it." In a more contemplative mood a woman participant reflected, "I feel very much at home here. Close to God. Very comfortable."

Focus group participants reinforce the message that divine energy is a part of their church experience. "One of the things that impressed me most about the church when I first came here on a Sunday morning was the fact that I found a worshiping people. You get a sense that you are directing yourself to God as opposed to just singing a friendly hymn to each other," was a comment in one focus group.

Sensing the energy of God in people's action, another person explained, "People are looking at people and ministries in this church and saying, 'I see God, and I see Jesus Christ in your actions. You are living the faith.' It isn't just lip service. I mean it's really happening here."

Clearly, God is at the center for the 14 churches studied for this research. Faith is focused on the Creator and Redeemer of the universe. There is a consistent connection between placing one's faith in God and being a part of the church's active concerns. But involvement in church alone does not equate to a commitment to God. One participant put it in just those terms: "It's not as much a commitment to your church as it is a commitment to God."

Reflecting on his own spiritual journey, in his book *Meeting Jesus Again for the First Time,* theologian Marcus Borg summarizes the reality of God for people who are involved in Future Faith churches: "God was no longer a concept or an article of belief, but ... an element of experience."[3] Expressing a similar deepening appreciation and love for Jesus in his book, *The Jesus I Never Knew,* noted evangelical author Philip Yancey concludes that Jesus "brought God near. To Jews who knew a distant, ineffable God, Jesus brought the message that God cares for the grass of the field, feeds the sparrows, numbers the hairs on a person's head. To Jews who dared not pronounce the Name (of God), Jesus brought the shocking intimacy of the Aramaic word, 'Abba.' – a familiar term of family affection equivalent to Daddy."[4] Faith that includes affection for God is part of the experience for people in Future Faith churches.

Communities that Inspire Confidence

Christian churches have reputations for telling bad news before they release the good news. In the conventional order of finding faith, first one needs to acknowledge the sin problem. When the sequence is right, repentance is expressed. Then and only then is God's forgiveness granted. It makes sense, after all, that confession and regret should precede the unmerited gift of salvation.

In the vast majority of the 14 churches, the order is less explicit and the lines are not as clearly drawn. Instead, human brokenness is assumed, including a broken relationship with God. These churches simply presume that everyone is in continual need of God's presence and intervention.

BELIEF IN A POSITIVE GOSPEL

Whether it is a deliberate choice to ignore negative messaging or an instinctive response to the dynamics of the modern world, Future Faith churches are not focusing on the dark side of life. Instead, they express confidence in the power of the positive gospel.

Without scripting the bad news, Future Faith churches emphasize the good news.

Without spelling out the specific sin, when people's spiritual lives are off track they are invited to get back on track with God. Instead of a lecture or an exhortation, if people are traveling away from God, Future Faith churches assume that God's ways are unarguably good ways. The natural response is to invite people to start traveling in God's direction again.

Our focus groups again provided illustrations of a positive gospel pattern. For example, a focus group in a Baptist church concluded that the emphasis in their church was "thou shalt" rather than "thou shalt not."

To delve deeper into the positive gospel, we asked several focus groups if their churches stood up against anything, or if any behavior or situation ever got denounced?

"I can't think of anything that is preached against," said a Baptist participant. An Anglican worshiper explained that "the emphasis is on the good news of forgiveness and acceptance. No matter what you've done, no matter where you are, you're accepted and from that point on we've got good news for you." Picking up on the same theme, a Catholic individual concluded, "It is the difference between 'I *get* to,' rather than, 'I *got* to'."

There are both strengths and vulnerabilities in every approach. Focusing on the positive dimensions of the faith is appealing and certainly compatible with the spirit of the age. However, Ron Sider offers an appropriate caution: "I get uncomfortable whenever I see people who profess to be Christians growing complacent with sin. Whether it's an issue of personal immorality (marital infidelity, for example) or corporate immorality (unfair labor practices, for another example), followers of Christ ought to abhor wrongdoing. In fact, Jesus and his new community of disciples challenged evil wherever they found it."[5]

BELIEF IN A RELEVANT FAITH

Experienced faith is a relevant faith. When the human spirit is in touch with God's spirit, the presence of the divine is personal and undeniable.

Etched into the soul of our sample churches is a nurturing belief in Jesus Christ that is relevant. Speaking about church leadership, one focus group participant said, "The first thing that struck me was they talked on a faith level that was my level. Not way up there – somebody talking to God that I had not an understanding of, or that I had no intimacy with."

Future Faith churches pass the relevance test in two distinct areas. In the present cultural mood, what affects "my experience" is both valid and valued. It was well put by the focus group participant who said, "I wasn't looking for community but for answers, and listening to the sermons really opened my eyes to a lot of things." Affirming the importance of a personal relationship with Jesus Christ results in people experiencing God.

The second realm of relevance in these times is best expressed by the slogan "what works has worth." When people get involved in responding to specific people in their communities, their action affirms the theory of their faith. Addressing moral, social, and vocational issues from the pulpit and in other forums builds people's confidence in the gospel. Pointing toward answers for people's struggles in our modern world created relevance for the participant who stated, "In the sermon, there will be different passages from the Bible but they will always bring it to everyday life."

Faith that works is relevant faith. It is in touch with realities of day to day life.

BELIEF IN HUMAN POTENTIAL AND HUMAN BROKENNESS

We noted earlier that many churches use bad news as a setup for telling the good news of the gospel. We acknowledged the rationale for getting the order right. If sinners are going to be redeemed, they need to be rescued from the mess they are in. One consequence of this line of logic however, is that Christian churches are often perceived to be "down on people."

By contrast, contemporary shapers of society lean more in the direction of being "up on people." Since the 1960s, psychologists, management gurus, popular writers and speakers like Leo Buscaglia, all have preached the promise of the human potential movement. New Age proponents have similarly elevated the human capacity to do great things. Belief in the principle of progress and the ability to solve problems is predicated on the magnificence of human ability. Under the surface, the drive and desire to build up self-esteem is rooted in an assumption of human worth and the inherent goodness and potential in people.

The diversity of the church has produced both views. And both, taken to an extreme, can be harmful. "Down on people" churches regularly remind their congregants that they are sinful and selfish. When taken to excess, people start feeling that they are worthless pieces of human wreckage. They readily confess "I can do nothing in my own strength. Without Christ I am nothing."

In contrast, "up with people" churches regularly remind their people that they are created in the image of God. They are invited to appreciate their created beauty, multitude of gifts, and inherent goodness. When you are created in the image of God, you have the capacity to grow more like God. These churches can drive home the narcissism of modern culture until people start believing that they are number one, no matter what.

"We're learning to follow. None of us is there."

Future Faith churches, in our findings, tend to embrace both views of people. They believe in both human potential and human brokenness. At the same time, they live with the tension of dealing with human strength and human weakness.

Talking about a pastor who affirmed human potential, a participant confided that the pastor doesn't feel threatened by letting people celebrate their strengths. He is "confident enough in the things that he does that he allows other people who have visions, who have dreams, who have gifts, to use them."

From the leadership side, Pastor David Watt captures the spirit of seeing potential in people. He illustrates from his favorite Bible passage, when Jesus comes to the pool of Bethesda. Jesus sees the paralyzed man who has been there for 38 years. Watt explains how this passage models ministry for him: "Jesus sees the man and reaches down to him and lifts him up and restores him. He sends him on his way to be a responsible person. That's the Jesus that captured my heart."

But acknowledging the human brokenness side of life is part of the Future Faith equation too. A United Church member estimates that "nine times out of ten our sermons are pastoral. People can find healing here; otherwise they cannot reach out and serve the community. People have to be healed to serve."

Speaking out of his experience in the Christian Reformed Church, another participant confirmed the need for pastoral care and healing. "I've had opportunity to pray with people who are broken," he said. "Following up with these people, they feel there was a place they could come to when they were broken. They were hurting, they had a need, and this church, through whatever means they found, provided for them."

One parishioner summarized the spirit of Future Faith churches when he said, "We're learning to follow. None of us is there. There's really no final stage. I guess we all strive for it, but we're not expected to be perfect. We're all learning, trying, stumbling, helping each other up."

In an intriguing fashion, these churches are retaining a commitment to orthodoxy and traditional Christian assumptions about the need for redemption. However, they are doing so without putting great emphasis on condemnation. There is ambiguity in the picture. People seem to be saying "We are sinful, but we are not inherently bad."

The spirit in the Future Faith churches coincides with the insight of C.S. Lewis:

No amount of falls will really undo us if we keep on picking ourselves up each time. We shall of course be very muddy and tattered children by the time we reach home. But the bathrooms are all ready and the towels put out, and the clean clothes in the airing cupboard. The only fatal thing is to lose one's temper and give it up. It is when we notice the dirt that God is most present in us: it is the very sign of His presence.[6]

Living with the dual reality of human weakness and human strength provides a strong foundation for the divine-human partnership that is the essence of church life. In divine terms, churches exist to connect people to God. In human terms, churches are places for people to express their gifts, care for others, and learn to live as disciples of Christ.

BELIEF IN DIVINE INTERVENTION

Retaining a view of human brokenness leads naturally to the need for divine intervention. Future Faith churches not only expect God to be present but also to intervene. A Presbyterian focus group expressed these expectations candidly when a participant said, "The Holy Spirit is here. I can sense it, that's why I stayed. There was deadness in the church I left. It was like the Holy Spirit had up and left. The spirit is at work here." A participant from a Vineyard church shared a similar perspective. For him the presence of God should be noticeable in the church. "It's noticeable when you walk through the doors on Sunday morning," he says, then adds, "It's noticeable even when there's nobody in the building." And a participant in the Aboriginal congregation mentioned that "what makes the worship services is that each time we come we expect to hear from God. The Holy Spirit moves in someone's life".

Certainly that sense of expectation is part of what a Catholic participant suggests is key. He described how he sees God becoming present to individuals: "If people want to encounter God, the presence of Christ, read scripture and celebrate the sacrament … there's a removal of obstacles here." And an Anglican churchgoer explained that she and her husband think God is "very present in the lives and in the ministry of people."

The spirit in the Future Faith churches aligns well with the experience of the Roman Catholic Church of St. Augustine and St. Paul in Washington, DC. During one Sunday service, before the time for passing the peace the priest said, "It would be a shame to leave here without knowing those around." But then he paused and said slowly, "It would be a much greater shame to leave here without knowing God." This statement was followed by extended applause. It was as if people were telling God, who they felt was in their presence, that they had no intention of leaving without knowing God.[7]

Involvement in church without expecting God to intervene is like going to work without receiving a pay cheque. An important part of the exchange is absent. In Future Faith churches the presence and activity of God is assumed and experienced.

Communities in which To Grow

The flow of life between God and the people in the identified churches is resulting in growth – organizational growth and personal spiritual growth. Increasing numbers of people are participating, and those who are involved are developing spiritually. One participant insightfully commented, "Our church was like a family that starts having children. They buy a house and they keep on having children and then have to buy a bigger house. That's exactly the way it is here. And God always provided what we needed to build on."

PLACES TO BELONG

The complexities of life in the modern world are creating a hunger for relationships and for places to belong. For reasons often related to the economy, mobility uproots people when they least expect it. Technology nurtures a hunger for the human touch – especially when voice mail puts you on hold, bank machines have no voice to hear or face to see, and e-mail preempts talking in person. Divorce and remarriage, re-engineering and downsizing in the workplace, unrelenting and uncontrolled change and uncertainty about the future, all make us feel fragile. The cumulative effect results in our want-

Involvement in organized religious life leads to a sense of personal belonging.

ing to hear the sound of our names. We want to belong somewhere and to be missed when we are not there.

There should be no surprise, then, that relationships abound in Future Faith churches. One focus group participant announced, "This is my home. This is my extended family, and it's a wonderful place to be. I feel I belong here." Other comments reiterate the same theme. "There is a strong sense of a family at this church and I feel supported in my search to understand God," said an Anglican congregant.

The sense of family is building a place of nurture for many individuals. A focus group participant described her church a "caring, nurturing family." She explained: "Because of the family focus here it means we fight together, we cry together, but we get up and we stick it out." One Mennonite Brethren participant summarized the sentiments of many, "The thing that we couldn't get over was the love that is here."

When the biblical ideal of church is experienced, involvement in organized religious life leads to a sense of personal belonging. Church is a place to feel safe among people who help sustain each other's weary spirits. As a cherished community for the faithful, it is also where we go when we desire to hear the sound of our names said with a genuine affection, or to touch and be touched. When church is working right, we are infused with life and we grow. We go deeper into Christ and his ways and become more like we are meant to be.

PLACES OF RESPECT

Respect is based on a reciprocal equation. If you don't give it, you don't receive it. The challenge is to find places and interact with people who are ready to both give and receive.

Obviously, it doesn't happen all the time in Future Faith churches, but there is a pattern. Rather than demanding conformity and compliance, these churches are places of mutual respect.

We heard the importance of respect from many focus groups. A woman told us, "One of the things that struck me the very first time was the respect they show for children here. And I don't have children." Another man enthusiastically talked about how his pastor extends respect. "Our minister doesn't say to you, 'I've discovered God, haven't you?'" He explains further that the pastor "respects where you are and he doesn't exclude you in how he talks. I never feel like he's talking down to us."

Places of mutual respect bring the best out of people. They engender a regard for others and nurture a healthy view of oneself. They also empower people.

PLACES OF EMPOWERMENT

Empowerment sends messages that encourage people to risk. Without fanfare, environments that empower extend "I believe in you" signals. They build confidence by indicating in many ways, "You have something important to offer."

People who are empowered grow. One participant gave an example of an empowering ministry, where a collective kitchen and bake shop is run in conjunction with the food bank. Women who come to the food bank are also helped by learning how to cook and stretch their food budget as well.

A complementary comment about the "people empowering side" of Future Faith churches explained, "Working in your passion, in your giftedness, that is very upbuilding. Very upbuilding." Belief in human giftedness is not limited to one denominational view of the faith. A Baptist churchgoer put it this way, "Take people where they are. Part of the excitement of ministry is allowing people to use whatever they have and watching them grow." And a United Church attender said, "I think that everyone has a ministry and that God calls everyone into ministry." A Vineyard member agreed when she noted, "We encourage people to dream, and as long as they are not theologically aberrant or immoral and don't ask for money, they can do what they want – and we'll help them."

To believe one is fully finished closes the door on change and the possibility of improvement.

Catholic theologian Karl Rahner speaks eloquently on empowerment when he describes Christianity as hope. He says it is through the "liberating contemplation of the crucified and risen Christ" that we come to know what is meant when we say "God." That understanding, or as he calls it essential of Christianity, "can't stay at the level of theory in people's heads or of Sunday sermons, but has to become life-immediate, realistic, and habitual – at the heart of the 'secular' daily round."[8]

PLACES TO CHANGE

Whether we are serious Christians or uncertain agnostics, whether we are female or male, employed or unemployed, to be a human being is to feel unfinished. To believe one is fully finished closes the door on change and the possibility of improvement. To conclude that one is unable to change or improve is to exclude an energizing God.

Future Faith churches both accept the reality of the unfinished and live with the expectation of change. In one Future Faith church a person commented that "The sermons really make you think about the way you're acting or the way you are running your life and what changes you need to make."

Reflecting a value change from an appetite for the fine things of this world to a desire for the things of God, one woman participant smiled and said, "My favorite store isn't Birks anymore. It's Christian book stores."

Change is the natural consequence when God inspires new life in spiritually-seeking people. When individuals expect next year to be like last year, they forfeit the chance to change, and they begin to die. When organizations plan to be the same yesterday, today, and tomorrow, they too begin to die. They forfeit their role and influence with succeeding generations. In churches, when vision fades, pews start to empty and buildings are eventually sold.

Communities with Expectations

Future faith churches live in the present with expectations for an enhanced future. And those expectations are linked directly to their belief that God is active, and that their people are gifted for ministry. The majority of the churches in the sample are more people-focused than they are program-driven. A focus group participant explained why this was important to him and his family: "I've moved frequently. The first and foremost test that we've used when we've moved into town, is to find a church not representing a denominational outlook but one that has a heart for ministry. One that helps people recognize what their gifts are and allows them to use them in ministry. That to me is the most important thing that I find in this church.

GIFTS TO SERVE

A lay person communicated good sense and solid theology with the perspective that "I go back to the parable of the talents … I had to come to grips with the idea that I didn't have ten talents. But I was responsible for one or two. So it's a question of does the church have the wisdom and the maturity and the ability to recognize that some people have lesser gifts than others? And does the church give people the opportunity to use and improve what they have?"

When churches function with the belief that congregants have gifts to offer in ministry to the God they desire to serve, life flourishes. Instead of today looking like yesterday, newness propels the present into a sustained future. Rather than dead end mentalities controlling the group, new doorways are opened into unexplored territory.

MISSIONS TO OWN AND DREAMS TO PURSUE

The expression of spiritual gifts incites spiritual visions and spiritual dreams – especially when the laity both own and participate in the ministry. A liberated and mandated laity are center stage in Future Faith churches. One liberated voice said, "We are not bound by the fact that it's only the ideas which originated in the cloistered halls of the ordained pastors or clerical staff that are allowed to be implemented. *We* are the church."

A lay person with vision and a clear philosophy of ministry suggests that rather than "have a bunch of programs established and trying to plug people into those programs and misusing individuals' times because it's not their passion," a good program will "get people to serve where they're gifted … If you have a new vision, and say 'This is my passion, why don't we start something new here?' we go for it. And that's the whole idea of how you begin to impact your city."

When lay vision partners with clergy leadership, the status quo is challenged. And a shared sense of mission generates dreams of what the divine-human partnership can create.

PROGRESS COEXISTS WITH PROBLEMS

For the purposes of researching this book, the criteria for choosing Future Faith churches included several factors.

- Their spiritual vital signs are strong and healthy.
- As congregations, they are growing numerically. They are communities of faith where many of the people who attend are developing spiritually.
- They foster reputations for inviting people to experience personal faith.
- They motivate their participants to be involved in ministries of social concern.

Still, these churches are not perfect. They all have problems to address. Their marks of progress coexist with lurking problems. In pursuit of godliness, Future Faith churches are very human places. The following excerpts are drawn from the full range of churches in the sample – mainline, evangelical and Catholic.

- "This church has gone through tough times where a lot of people left. They didn't like the choices that were being made … I think the people who have stayed with this church over the years are those who can accept other people and in the face of disagreement know when to say 'Well, those aren't really the essentials of my faith and the Lord is still working.'"

In this life, only graveyards are tidy.

- "This church is a human entity. It consists of a lot of human beings who have struggles. I mean no one said that being Christian is going to be easy. There are a lot of issues, a lot of burdens here, but it's still a pretty good church."

- "In the congregation there are differences. I've always found opportunity to air those differences. People are quite open to that. We've aired out differences about the music team and I've gone away somewhat satisfied because at least we've been heard."

- "We worked through the issue of the music minister whose philosophy of ministry was light years away from anybody else in the church. That was actually a unifying thing as we worked it through in a positive way. He realized that we didn't really have the same philosophy of ministry, so there was a mutual parting of ways. We still have a good relationship with him. But that was necessary for the whole church to go ahead."

- "My first impression was that there was a very intense ownership of the church. There were many, many positive things to be said about it. But the church had experienced 5 years of conflict mainly around two individuals. The conflict is still there. My approach to it was a kind of "I don't know anything about this. I wasn't here during the major conflict. I wasn't a part of it. My focus was not on let's fix this now."

- "Growth has created some facility problems and economic problems for us. I will continue to be disappointed if our church does not try to come to grips with the facilities problems. We have already lost some excellent people who could have given leadership. But the facilities will have a lot to do with how long we are able to continue to offer these programs. Everybody in the church is invited to discuss all aspects of the ministry. We have got to be open and have honest discussion. But some people will be upset whether we choose to build or not to build."

Life after death may be problem free. In this life, only graveyards are tidy. Even in churches that evidence strong spiritual vital signs there are problems and difficulties. The good news is that in the midst of problems, progress prevails.

COMMITMENTS FROM THE SOUL

Future Faith churches are threading their way through the maze of the modern world. Captured by a strong sense of the reality of God and a concern to care for others, they are in touch with God and responding to the social needs of people around them. As communities of grace they are places of soul care. As communities of growth they are motivating their people to express social care.

In the larger picture of the contemporary church, the soul of the church is still divided. One-sided faith polarizes the personal from the social. The importance of "loving God" is frequently transmitted on a single frequency. A separate signal is sent on the "love your neighbor" frequency. On one side there are churches that are "fervently committed to the task of world evangelism and wanting to see heaven populated with redeemed individuals. On the other side are those whose hearts break for hurting humanity where oozing emotional and physical sores are graphic reminders of the flawed condition of the human soul."[9]

Future faith churches embrace both sides of the God and neighbor equation. They believe in heaven and in life after death. But they also believe in life after birth. They have a vision for heaven on earth on this side of the grave.

Still, we have to acknowledge that in the more normative state of church affairs "conservative religion has become pre-occupied with words and dogma. Correct religious language has replaced an emphasis upon faithful action. Personal piety has become an end in itself instead of the energy for social justice. Religious language has little or no connection to moral action in society."[10]

On the other side, too often "liberal religion has lost its spiritual center. It has become both reactive to conservative religion and captive to the shifting winds of secular culture. Liberal activism has often lacked any real dynamic of personal conversion, and therefore, transformative power. With liberal religion, social action in the world can be severed from its roots in faith, producing a language and practice that seem more bureaucratic and ideological than spiritual."[11]

Tragically, conservative religion has lost any sense of biblical breadth and surrendered to pragmatic and theological reductionism. It too has become both reactive to liberal religion and captive to individualism and church growth techniques. Conservative religion advocates have lacked compassion for those who do not see life as they see it. With conservative religion, personal faith can be severed from God's concern for justice and the earthly needs of the poor and the marginalized. Personal piety can produce the form of godliness without the power of the risen Christ to transform the dread of today into a more beautiful and hopeful tomorrow.

Out of the soul of Future Faith churches come two appeals. "Mainline churches should not abandon their courageous stand against racism, economic injustice, and oppression, but they do need to ground their social action in solid biblical orthodoxy. And they need to become as enthusiastic about leading lost sinners to Christ as they are about liberating the oppressed of the earth."[12]

Conservative churches, similarly, should not abandon their bold and unrelenting call to personal salvation, but they need to ground their vision for personal faith in solid biblical orthodoxy. They need to become as enthusiastic about liberating the oppressed on earth as they are about leading lost souls to Christ.

Deep in the inner spirits of God's committed people there is a sense that when Jesus was on planet earth he "never struggled with such compartmentalization. Demonstrating compassion and simultaneously seeking the conversion of the heart were irrevocably welded and intertwined in the mind and ministry of the Son of God."[13]

When the contemporary church and the people of God are more like Jesus, then the gospel can be whole and the people of God can be fully Christian.

3

DISCERNING THE SOUL OF
FUTURE FAITH LEADERS

Effective church leaders create waves. Like pebbles thrown
into a pond, they make ripples which affect the life of the
church in ever widening circles. Some leaders are like big
rocks that send splashing waves in their wake. Others are
more like smooth stones that skip across the surface leaving
little evidence of their presence. Whether ripples or splashes,
the mood, atmosphere, and vibrancy of congregations across
the land are profoundly influenced by their leaders.

Our leadership interviews make one conclusion obvious.
Leaders need to be aware of the impact of their role and the
chain reaction of widening influence that their part plays in
the life of the church.

A pattern among the 14 leaders we interviewed also became predictable. Leaders work out their ministry from the
guts of their personal history. Who the leader is and how he
or she approaches life becomes the "stuff" from which these
people lead. Self-understanding is crucial.

THE INSIDE STORY OF LEADERS

During one of my [Gary's] seminary classes on preaching, the professor asked, "What is preaching? What is it all about?" The students, caught up in the heady air of ideas and concepts, eagerly returned answers bloated with theological ideas and academic terminology. The professor eventually brought the students down to earth. He listened patiently before providing a simple but profound answer: "Preaching is simply God's story in your story."

Our research and dialogue with pastoral leaders across Canada takes the professor's response one step further. All leaders find their effectiveness when they *understand* God's story in their story. Personal biography shapes the way leaders lead. And people in the pews respond to leaders they perceive to be genuine and transparent.

In previous generations, the clergy office brought with it a certain amount of respect and authority. Jeff Woods writes, "A local church pastor was among the most respected and educated people within a community ... Everyone wanted to get on the good side of the local pastor. That is hard to give up. For many, there will be no choice. It will be taken away."[1]

Today trust and influence are garnered from what people perceive, know, and believe the leader to be. According to Mike Regele, "Authority in the future will be granted to people, not to positions. It will not be enough, and indeed will most likely be counterproductive, to claim authority based upon position."[2]

A general distrust of all public figures today has created different qualities that congregational members expect from a minister in the 1990s. People sitting in the pew today look for a quality of relationship that provides a window into the life of the clergy and which allows them to trust their minister's words.

At Deer Park United Church in Calgary, Jennifer Ferguson and John Pentland provide this kind of Future Faith leadership. A focus group participant from their congregation remarked, "Many times we hear Jennifer and John crack a joke or laugh up there on the platform. I mean, they are human."

Personal biography shapes the way leaders lead.

A woman at Six Nations Pentecostal Church in Ontario told us that her pastor had a similar leadership style. She said, "I believe the scripture where the Lord said that he would give us pastors according to his own heart. I look at Pastor Dan and I can see that in him. I know that as a body we need to continue to hold him up before God because he really does have struggles and trials just like anybody else."

The same sentiment came from a focus group participant in Vancouver. She says the pastoral staff at Willingdon Church "present themselves as people that make mistakes and are willing to admit that. They put themselves in a vulnerable position."

This new reality requires leaders who understand and are able to share their story. They are people who have touched life and have not deceived themselves about what they are about and who they are becoming.

It's a tough task. Eugene Peterson believes that pastoral leaders are easily deceived. He writes, "Deception is nowhere more common than in religion. And the people most easily and damningly deceived are the leaders."[3] If clergy are unaware of the themes that motivate their own lives and ministry, that self-deception or lack of self-awareness can play itself out in the life of the congregation.

Our research reveals that Future Faith congregations are looking for transparency and trustworthy character in their leaders. They seek to be led by leaders who understand life and are vulnerable in their relationships. Rather than revering preachers in positions lifted up six feet above contradiction, the folks in the pews are responding to real people.

VULNERABLE AND TRANSPARENT

Honest biographies are not all stories of triumph. The clergy we interviewed were open about their disappointments and honest about their struggles. Most were aware of how the pain in their lives had served as a transformational factor in the way they acted as leaders.

This self-knowledge of painful histories results in more compassionate leadership. Richard Higginson observes that "often we learn more from failure than we do from the experience of success." The reasons are simple. He says, "We take success more easily for granted. We do not stop and analyze the reasons why we have been successful. Failure makes us stop and work out what went wrong."[4]

Whether it was a failure or a profound life-changing experience, the leaders studied in our research used those moments to move forward and learn. It altered the way they perceived themselves and the way they entered their leadership task.

Father Corbin Eddy at Ottawa's Saint Basil's Roman Catholic Church described his life with transparency. "Our family was dysfunctional. My father was an alcoholic: He wasn't wild, aggressive, nasty and abusive – just passive. We grew up in a small town and he was a very influential person and all three of us kids went away to school when we were 13 or 14. When I got out of that situation I became aware that the way I grew up was not particularly normal. But all of that has caused me to be more flexible and open. My background has a lot to do with that."

Difficult life events are the single most crucial factor in allowing leaders to be more human and genuine in their life as clergy leaders. Understanding how these events have shaped their living ultimately results in genuineness and authentic caring for others. Future Faith leaders know what their limitations are and are willing to show them. They are aware of the ambiguities and struggles of their own lives. As a result, they see others differently.

Wounded people who forgive and heal without becoming bitter can help other wounded people heal too.

Dan Doolittle, pastor of Six Nations Pentecostal Church, lives a life that illustrates this truth. "The day I realized I was out of control, I told my wife she better call her pastor … That pastor stayed around my bed and prayed for 16 hours … God did set me free."

Doug Ward from Kanata Baptist Church recalls a pastoral situation which almost caused him to quit. But as he reflects on his ministry and call, Doug points out that "one of the peculiar things about a pastor is that so much of your own person is caught up with the calling. You've been trained for this, and you're going to die in this. But you get too caught up in that and watch yourself being damaged. I was not able to make that distinction. A couple of friends bailed me out. They pointed out to me that I needed to get out of that situation and reinvest my call. They are still some of my best friends at this period in my life."

The good news is that wounded people who forgive and heal without becoming bitter can help other wounded people heal too.

CONFESSIONAL AND HONEST

Knowing your story, and recognizing God in it, creates the self-awareness that Doug Ward demonstrates. It's a self-awareness that builds an honest and transparent environment from which leaders can work.

In Winnipeg, Paul Wartman gives leadership at The Meeting Place. He is confessional and vulnerable when talking about his own journey: "I think one of the things that breathed life into me occurred when I stopped playing games of pretense and began to be more honest about who I am – my pride, my weakness, my vulnerability."

A woman from St. Basil's Catholic Church repeated the same story that her priest, Corbin Eddy, had told us in his interview. "When he is talking about his dysfunctional family I think, 'Oh, thank goodness, I am not the only one.' He will say that in front of the congregation and you really feel a rapport with him when he is talking to you."

Confessional leadership establishes a model for a community that can also be vulnerable and open. Mutual sharing takes place and people in the church community become influencers in the leader's life. Confessional leaders are both "shapers" and are shaped by the community of faith they serve.

Future Faith leaders do not come with a pre-packaged plan that must be bought by the congregation. The ups and downs of their own journey predispose them to expect similarly variable patterns in their parishioners. They are willing to share themselves in the discovery of what it means to be the church together. Their vulnerability gives permission for others to live transparently as a community of people and to discover together what faith can mean for them as a congregation.

A focus group member at Oakridge Presbyterian Church in London, Ontario, described the way their clergy live confessionally among the congregation. "Terry and Peter are real. They are ready to laugh at themselves. They talk about their foibles and their mistakes and become relevant to us. They are not standing up there preaching at us. They are walking as if they were in our shoes too. I think the fact they are able to do this says, 'I have been there'."

Barry Parker, the Rector at St. John's the Evangelist Anglican Church in Edmonton, articulates the same message: "For the modern pastor there are non-negotiables – things like integrity, vulnerability and transparency. They are absolutely critical."

BELIEVING IN PEOPLE AND THEIR POTENTIAL

One of those anonymous quotes you sometimes find stuck up in the private space of a colleague's work area reads, "If you want to know who a person is, do not ask what he does but what he loves." The quote illustrates the focused reality of many church leaders. They have a passion for people simply because they value people. "You're not a nobody, you're a somebody" is the slogan David Watt uses to describe his attitude toward people and the atmosphere of fellowship which permeates the life of First Baptist Church, Dartmouth.

It's more than just oneness. These leaders have taken pains to know their own story and they take care to know their congregation as well. Father Corbin Eddy says with emphasis, "If we don't take advantage of every person who is ready to participate and ready to offer something, then we are the losers." This understanding comes from the deep belief that everyone's participation is important.

This theme was raised consistently as we talked with clergy. Jennifer Ferguson of Deer Park United Church said, "I think that everyone has a ministry. People want to know what their

God-given gifts are and how to put them into practice." Doug Ward reflected on the changes that have happened to him over his years of pastoral ministry. He said, "I have a much deeper trust in my people now than I used to have." That combination of trust coupled with knowledge of people's life-stories will enable a leader to show the congregation that each individual is important to what is done in and by the church. At Kelowna Vineyard Church, this is a founding principle. Wesley Campbell told us, "We encourage people to dream any dream they have, and do it. As long as you are theologically grounded – do what you want."

While it took a different shape in every congregation, these leaders seemed to hold a deep conviction about the worth of people within their congregations. Parishioners are not "pawns" to be manipulated, and they are not to be distrusted. The leaders we interviewed echoed Martin Luther King's wise statement: "Whom you would change you must first love."[5]

Future Faith leaders listen and learn from the people of their congregation. Terry Ingram relates this leadership task to the creation and development of congregational life by asserting, "If people feel that they have been heard and taken seriously, they'll let you get away with a lot." He goes even further to contend, "You have to trust both the people and the process."

LIVING COMFORTABLY WITH THE UNFINISHED

"An accepting community is critical," says Harold Percy, who gives leadership in Trinity Anglican Church in Streetsville, Ontario. He tells people, "This is a community for people just like you. You won't shock us; you're welcome here as you are." He urges church communities wherever they are to develop intentionally an accepting atmosphere for people to explore their spirituality. With his characteristic turn of phrase he concludes, "We try to be a Velcro church instead of a Teflon church. We want them [newcomers] to get caught here. Over time, as we open doorways and opportunities, they'll find a place to raise their questions and meet their needs."

There must also be a desire to move beyond just mere acceptance.

Just as Future Faith leaders are not afraid to relate to others, neither are they afraid to wait for the unfinished in people's lives. They are aware of the unfinished nature of their own lives. They are not threatened by the complexity and ambiguity of present-day living. David Watt observes from his 37 years of ministry: "I can't be shocked any more. I think early in my ministry I was too judgmental. But I think you change – time and time again. If you hang in there with people, the day comes when they change too."

This acceptance is first modeled by leaders and then translated into a mood of acceptance in the church. We heard many people describe their church the way Mike Rietsma described First Christian Reformed of Calgary. "This place is known as a safe place where people can come and they don't have to be perfect. They can have warts that show. We have a reputation of willingness to accept and to receive people with their problems."

Extending acceptance is only one edge of community life. There must also be a desire to move beyond just mere acceptance.

Future Faith leaders require a vision for what can be. It is a difficult thing to walk a double-edged framework of acceptance and challenge, and these leaders are aware of that danger. They find themselves in tension between the prophetic and the priestly roles of ministry. The prophetic side of pastoral ministry sets the boundaries of what God is calling us to. The priestly side of pastoral ministry brings people into an atmosphere of grace and forgiveness.

Susan Howatch, in her novel *Absolute Truths,* describes these two aspects of ministry. The main character of her novel, an Anglican priest, challenges himself when he asks, "There were two aspects to Christ's ministry, weren't there? The prophetic and the pastoral: he spoke out against sin but at the same time he behaved with compassion toward sinners. And he held those two aspects of ministry in perfect balance. But I haven't. I've emphasized the prophetic at the expense of the pastoral."[6]

Balance between these tensions is difficult to attain. John Cougar Mellancamp writes in a song, "I've seen the balance, I see it every time I swing by."[7] It is our belief after these interviews with leaders and focus groups that the pastoral ability to be accepting of the unfinished while envisioning growth and change can be held in dynamic tension. The prophetic quality of ministry maintains a vision for the finished in the midst of the unfinished, and for the unfinished in the midst of the finished. The pastoral ministry creates the atmosphere from which the prophetic can be heard.

Father Corbin Eddy echoes this sentiment. "I try to communicate to everybody that life isn't a problem to be solved; it's an ongoing adventure." He observes that part of the leadership task is "to spark the religious imagination and to put people in various situations that might be different from the situations that they have actually experienced so far. To help them realize that most of our limitations come from lack of experience."

Leaders like this have a faith edge because they use the tension between the pastoral and prophetic to energize ministry. They all convey the same passion for people mixed with the possibility that all people can be more than they realize. Presbyterian Terry Ingram exemplifies this attitude when he says, "I want to encourage people to be receptive to what God is doing in their lives. Hopefully I have the grace to back off and trust God's spirit to do the rest."

VISION FOR DOUBLE-EDGED FAITH

Future Faith leaders also hold firmly to a double-edged gospel. Their commitment embraces both sides of the gospel injunction, to love God and to love your neighbor. They believe passionately that if the church is to be relevant in today's world it must have a double-edged faith. For the church to be both biblical and relevant, they must balance individual spirituality with social concern.

Christian Reform pastor Mike Rietsma ministers in Calgary and believes the gospel has the power to touch the entire complexity of life. Discussing the church and its mission he says, "It ought not only to be strong theologically and strong spiritually, but also strong in terms of action – social action." Recalling lessons he learned in another position with a Pentecostal congregation, he concludes, "You want to minister to the whole person – not just soul and spirit but to the body and the emotions – all of life."

Tim Dickau adds meaning to double-edged faith when he says, "To minister among the poor and the outsiders is not a program of ministry. It is to be incarnational. We invite people to journey together with God." Dan Doolittle explains incarnational ministry from his experience. Dan says when God gave his congregation a vision to start a food bank, "It grew out of the desire to show God's love. To show that God is a God of supply the same way that Jesus broke fish and fed everybody who was there."

This double-edged holistic ministry is "fleshed out" in these leaders' abilities to mobilize people, not only inside the church where they worship but also in the places where they live. While the church is the place where faith is experienced with others who are like-minded, the places they live are where the faith is practiced and made real.

It takes strong personal security for ministers to affirm a "ministry where you are" mindset. Most clergy leaders tend to find their meaning and identity in what happens inside the walls of the church. This often translates into mainte-nance of church programs rather than connectedness with the surrounding community.

Future Faith leaders can envision what needs to happen outside the church, and organize life inside the church ac-cordingly. They believe their members need to integrate their faith with life outside the walls of the church. "The church is most effective when everyone's out of this building," is the way Doug Ward describes it.

THE DISTINCTIVES OF CHRISTIANITY

Future Faith leaders believe that when people encounter God, the experience transforms both the believer and the community of faith. John Pentland works with Jennifer Ferguson at Deer Park United and describes how this hap-pens in their faith community. "People love stories. They love to know the spiritual stories of each other's lives and how that connects with their story. For a lot of our sermons, Jennifer and I tell the stories of people in the congregation. We include other people we encounter and then show how the biblical story and their stories are knit together." As a result the congregation experiences a "deeper intimacy and connecting with one another."

Churches are spiritually vibrant where they have pastoral leadership that unapologetically weaves the reality of God into the lives of people. Many writers and church analysts have suggested that when mainline or other churches have weak spiritual conviction, there

Truth must be a lived reality.

is also a weakening of community in their congregations. Some churches in the mainline tradition "have reduced the Christian faith to belief in God, and respect for Jesus and the Golden Rule; among this group a growing proportion have little need for the church." A lesson for all churches from the mainline experience of decline is to "address theological issues head on … to provide compelling answers to the question, 'What's so special about Christianity?'"[8]

Future Faith churches understand that the crucial difference relates to affirming the distinctives of the Christian faith. They understand that truth must be a lived reality in the way William Willimon and Stanley Hauerwas describe: "It is important for the church as witness to have something to say that is more interesting than what the world says. When church becomes Rotary, church will lose because Rotary serves lunch and meets at a convenient hour of the week."[9]

One focus group participant from Saint Basil's church in Ottawa describes their parish priest, Corbin Eddy, as someone who understands the need to take a distinctively Christian stand. She told us: "Corbin is a man of faith. He believes in God. Because he can see God in many things, he affirms the fact that we ourselves are capable of experiencing and discovering that God."

A true love of God fuels a true love of neighbor. The result is the pursuit of a double-edged faith that is dynamic both inside and outside the church walls.

This kind of Christian community transcends mere activism. The "care of the soul" dictates the depth of the action people initiate into the community around them. "It's not so much a technique," Presbyterian Terry Ingram says. "It's an environment we create – it's the spirit of the congregation." He goes further in emphasizing the need for a deep engagement with the Scripture. "There isn't any normative voice any more telling them what integration ought to look like. We have to trust and pray for the Spirit to do that for us." This involvement with scripture provides a natural place for soul encounters with God and for God to prepare people to encounter one another.

HEALTHY LEADERS LEAD TO HEALTHY CHURCHES

During the eighties, the role of the leader evolved. Secular research moved beyond measuring a leader by standards of management efficiency. The '80s leader also began to shape values, transform people, and keep goals before the organization. Stephen Covey, one of the management gurus, teaches that "the only person over whom you have direct and immediate control is yourself ... you must cultivate the habits of leadership effectiveness for yourself, and doing so will be the single best investment you'll ever make."[10]

This is by no means a new concept. The apostle Paul points this out in the beginning of his letter to the Thessalonians when he makes a crucial observation, "You also became imitators of us and of Christ Jesus" (1 Thessalonians 1:6). People imitate, clone, or absorb the character of their leaders. Future Faith leaders are not afraid to ask themselves: "What is it we want to have cloned?" They intentionally develop personal core values and belief characteristics that portray the kind of faith their communities want to identify with. They know these characteristics are first modeled in the leaders themselves.

Eugene Peterson helps us understand this when he states, "The way we learn something is more influential than the something that we learn. No content comes into our lives free-floating: it is always embedded in a form of some kind."[11] The way leaders model an integration of their personal encounter with God and their concern for social relevance is crucial to a congregation's ability to live out that integration. The real question is what kind of ripples does leadership produce?

LEADING FROM THE SOUL

In Canadian culture, leadership is often entered reluctantly. Jennifer Ferguson reflects the societal tension in which many Canadian clergy leaders feel trapped. "It's hard for me to talk about leadership when I feel I lead reluctantly," she says. Leadership, however, is a fundamental ingredient of effective church life that cannot be avoided. Loren Mead writes, "Clergy are a critical part of the problem. Many of them are uncomfortably aware of that fact."[12]

Perhaps they are uncomfortable because they realize what is required. Kirk Hadaway and David Rozen describe this discomfort. At an evangelism seminar they were discussing the changing face of clergy leadership. One clergy person reflected on his 30 years in the ministry and told them how things had changed. "To do ministry today, it is necessary to be a person of faith. Thirty years ago, all it took was being a professional."[13]

To become a leader who transforms congregations into spiritually dynamic communities, it is necessary for leaders to discern their own souls. Professional expertise is not enough; they must also be people of strong faith.

By living and leading from their soul, leaders in Future Faith churches reflect what Gordon Macdonald calls the be-low-the-waterline-issues of life. He writes, "The soul is the deeper part of all of us that others cannot see ... In that deeper, quiet piece of spiritual geography there was in biblical times and is today, dialogue with heaven, events of repentance, praise... and the formation of intentions to life and knowl-edge that enable people to become what I like to call king-dom builders."[14]

We see hints of the amazing capacities that God meant for leaders to possess. It is meant to be the product of the ind-welling Spirit of God that comes to replace the deadened parts of our own lives. Life below the waterline that is lived from the soul is just that – *life*.[15]

Future Faith leaders have plumbed the depth of their lives. They allow their souls to be nurtured by Word and Spirit so that they bring a unique depth and understand-ing of spirituality to the leadership task. Even secular man-agement consultants Lee Bolman and Terence Deal con-tend, "The signs point toward spirit and soul as the es-sence of leadership."[16]

If this soul reality is undervalued, the result is a hollow leader – a person who spends most of life and ministry sim-ply responding to events and circumstances rather than liv-ing through them.

Leading from the soul provides intangible, mysterious qualities of character that set Future Faith leaders apart. They are more than the sum total of managers, program direc-tors, and religious professionals. The spiritual quality of their souls generates a capacity to be transformational leaders. Without that capacity, church life is shallow and congrega-tional vitality is weak.

Anglican Harold Percy uses the term transformation to describe his task of ministry and
leadership: "I think what I do is hope, pray, and
work for transformation of character and transformation of personality. So I don't see myself
as a prophet in the way of denouncing some-

In Canadian culture, leadership is often entered reluctantly.

thing. I really see myself as pastor of evangelism. I encourage
people to see a better way to work in life, and I'm hoping that
somewhere through that long process people are transformed
and see the world in different ways."

CREATING THE RIGHT WAVES

Churches take on the character and values of their leadership. Leaders bring themselves to the task, and people model
what they see and experience in their leaders.

This understanding of leadership calls for "catalyst leaders" who are more than pastoral care-givers, more than counselors, more than managers. Warren Lai, pastor of the
Scarborough Chinese Church in Toronto, has a contagious
spirit and is explicit about his leadership role. "I would describe myself as a catalyst. I throw lots of exciting possibilities into the hearts of my people." Charles Van Engen observes, "Merely developing authority – only telling people
what they should do and devising programs to do it – will
not be enough to mobilize the people of God. The people
must be shown a model that presses them to *want* to achieve
those intentional missionary goals of the congregation."[17]

He goes on to contend that "the spiritual, emotional and
mental personhood of their leaders provides the *heart* of missionary congregations."[18]

Effective church leaders create waves. Out of the spiritually enriched souls of leaders flow ripples that find their way
into the heart of Future Faith churches.

4

STRATEGIES FOR FUTURE
FAITH LEADERS

After three years of seminary I [Gary] can now admit that I knew almost nothing about leadership. Not that leadership was ignored in courses; that is simply an observation about me. I never understood the role beyond the theory until I worked with an associate in my first full time pastoral role. During that time he demonstrated the difference between being a manager and leader.

My colleague became my mentor and friend. For five years we spent hours discussing the role of the clergy-leader. As a young seminary graduate who "knew everything," there were times that I felt at odds with what he fleshed out in the leadership role. Yet today, as pastoral leader of a downtown "Old First Church," I often realize, with a wry chuckle, that the words coming out of my mouth are words I have heard before – words spoken by a wise leader who modeled what ministry and leadership could be.

THE CHANGING FACE OF LEADERSHIP

Fortunately for me, my mentor personified the shift taking place at that time in pastoral ministry. Consultant Kennon Callahan describes that shift when he says that we must face the fact that "the day of the professional minister is over, the day of the missionary pastor has come." [1]

For years seminaries focused on passive models of congregational life. These models were framed around the basic assumption that people still came to church and that denominational identity was still part of the equation. To reverse the decline of local congregations, all that was required was simply "to do" church better.

Trapped in these faulty assumptions, churches struggled in the changing environment. They paid lip service to the new agendas of leadership, but the radical implications for the church were simply ignored. Efforts were made to retool the programs and redefine the role of the clergy. Clinical pastoral education, pastoral counseling, and many other well-intentioned programs trained the minister for service to church members. The leadership focus was inside the church, while the shift of society was away from the church. As a result, clergy increasingly found themselves equipped for a ministry that only touched the faithful remnant who still attended.

Pastoral ministry was conceived as happening inside the walls of the church and the denominational organization. Clergy became, at best, a pastoral caregiver and personal spiritual guide to the local congregation – at worst, a paid friend to members of the church.

Evangelical churches were not immune to this change. They sought to release laity for ministry, but the energy was too often focused solely on the internal life of the congregation rather than the broader mission of the church.

Except for the occasional foray of evangelistic endeavor, the liberation of the laity
tended to focus on internal church functions.

Quantitative church measurements became
the focus. The minister was perceived to be
the catalyst who provided the atmosphere for
numerical growth to take place. Still attempting to retool the church in the old framework,
the orientation was on attracting people into
the church rather than scattering the people
intentionally into the world. Unlike their main-

**Clergy
increasingly
found
themselves
equipped for a
ministry that
only touched
the faithful
remnant who
still attended.**

line sisters who slowly declined in this outreach-passive
framework, some evangelical churches continue to function
well in terms of the quantitative measurement, but unfortunately grew at the expense of other churches around them.

Harold Percy, the Director of Evangelism for Wycliffe
College in Toronto, articulates a new agenda for mission-
minded leadership. He contrasts the pastoral and the mission
driven parish or church. In Harold's analysis, the leadership
style in a pastoral parish is primarily managerial, seeking to
keep everything in order and running smoothly. The leadership style in a mission parish is primarily transformational,
casting a vision of what can be, and marching off the map in
order to bring the vision into reality. Illustrating the point,
Percy suggests:

The pastoral parish asks, "How many visits are being made?"
The mission parish asks, "How many disciples are being made?"
The pastoral parish says, "We have to be faithful to our past."
The mission parish says, "We have to be faithful to our future."
The pastoral parish thinks about how to save the church.
The mission parish thinks about how to reach the world.[2]

In the societal paradigm of the past, the pastoral model was effective simply because the majority of people in Canada attended church or had a brand-name loyalty to a specific denomination. While some Canadian churches will function effectively within the old "passive" mindset into the next decade, present realities and future trends will require most congregations and leaders to alter their course.

The new direction for leaders is framed by the responses the participants made in the leadership section of the questionnaire. A total of 418 respondents from Future Faith churches identified what they perceived to be the primary leadership style that best described how the senior pastor or main ministers of their church tend to lead. The results were definitive.

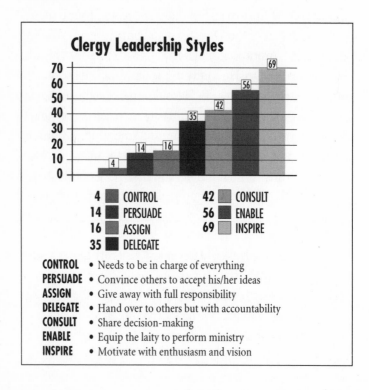

4	CONTROL	• Needs to be in charge of everything
14	PERSUADE	• Convince others to accept his/her ideas
16	ASSIGN	• Give away with full responsibility
35	DELEGATE	• Hand over to others but with accountability
42	CONSULT	• Share decision-making
56	ENABLE	• Equip the laity to perform ministry
69	INSPIRE	• Motivate with enthusiasm and vision

Inspiring, not Persuading

Future Faith leaders inspire others to participate and join them in their vision of a missionary church. A total of 69% of the congregational members stated that their leaders inspire them with enthusiasm and vision. In contrast, only 14% feel as if persuasion is used as a way to lead.

In our focus group discussions, we heard similar affirmations. One participant placed importance on the atmosphere the leader sets. He said that in his church individuals "are inspired and supported by an atmosphere that says 'Go for it.'"

Another participant explained how that atmosphere is developed. He said the thing he liked about his pastor was that "He is an idea person. I really appreciate talking to him because you can discuss Sunday school, mission and ministry, or other church activities and he has got great ideas, so he is inspiring." Similarly, another participant's pastor can "cast a vision and motivate people. He doesn't necessarily tell you what to do, but he has a way of motivating people."

Michael Armour and Don Browning, in their book *Systems-Sensitive Leadership*, describe this role by telling us, "If leaders fail in the role of vision-casting, nothing else can fill the void."[3] Inspirational leaders have a clear understanding of the values they hold and combine those values with a vision for how they will implement them. They build an intentional strategy that allows that vision to take place.

Defining leadership as "the capacity to create a compelling vision, translate it into action, and sustain it," Warren Bennis believes that "with vision, the leader provides the all-important bridge from the present to the future.[4] Working with entrepreneurial inclinations, they recognize that what others do is important and their enthusiasm for the vision creates an atmosphere of excitement that moves the congregation outward with increasing synergy.

Some leaders, however, are not always eager to accept the inspirational imperative. Perhaps this is motivated by the Canadian desire to be understated, or simply by the leader's natural uneasiness with the responsibility which derives from the inspirational agenda. The reluctance, however, is illustrated in marked differences of response between clergy and laity in the questionnaire. Of the clergy who participated in the questionnaire, only 50% felt that their role as inspirational catalysts was crucial to effective and healthy congregational life. On the other hand, 70% of the lay people felt that inspiring leadership was essential.

While some Future Faith leaders may be reluctant in the role of inspirer, they are all aware of its need. When asked how the people of the congregations they serve would describe their leadership style, one person answered, "I encourage people. So they get confidence, they believe anything's possible." Another person in leadership laid out priorities this way, "I don't care a hoot about buildings, or being a Christian cathedral, but I do care about reaching the lost."

In their love for a proof text, people in the church often quote Proverbs 29:18: "Where there is no vision, the people perish." Whether or not that is a precise translation from the Hebrew text, it points to an important truth – most people want to know where they are headed and will resist leaders who appear to be wandering aimlessly. They look for leaders to provide the road map for an enhanced future.

ARTICULATING A VISION

This ability to articulate vision becomes an empowering force for the church. Taking the natural reluctance of Canadians toward leadership and their tendency to remain as observers, these leaders create an atmosphere of enthusiasm and energy. Their inspirational leadership epitomizes Browning and Armour's five themes that must be addressed by leaders who cast a vision in any organization.

"If leaders fail in the role of vision-casting, nothing else can fill the void."

1. Leaders must have a clear picture in their own minds where the church is going.
2. They must identify the key strategies that will move the church from where it is to where it needs to be.
3. That vision and those strategies must become internalized in each leader's heart. They should come to mind immediately and succinctly every time a leader faces a consequential decision or is asked about congregational plans.
4. Leaders must work tirelessly to find simple, clear-cut ways in which to explain this vision and the strategies that support it.
5. Leadership must communicate, communicate, communicate to the congregation.[5]

FEELING INCLUDED

Whether intentionally or intuitively, Future Faith leaders inspire the people in their congregations. They provide both the atmosphere and the attitudes for congregational members to both encounter God and live out the implications of the faith they profess. They motivate soul care and social care for the ministry and service they envision.

People who participated in the research obviously see a difference between leaders who inspire and those who try to persuade and convince others. Only 14% of the participants saw persuasion as an effective leadership style. Leaders who use the heavy hand of persuasion in their desire to get things done are perceived as manipulative, pushy, and controlling. Inspiration, on the other hand, motivates people to function as adults. It provides an atmosphere of choice and participation which eliminates the possibility of feeling coerced or browbeaten. A focus group member described her minister. "He respects where you are and he doesn't exclude you." Another participant said, "They are the leaders here, they help facilitate things; but they do not have the ultimate last word."

Future Faith leaders are effective communicators who use that ability to motivate the members of their congregations. They draw from the pool the collective energies of the congregation in pursuit of common goals by inviting people into the process of vision casting and working with them toward an adoption of a shared cause. People who participate in this process feel empowered and included in the ministry that develops.

Enabling, not Controlling

Jennifer Ferguson described the discovery she and her husband, co-pastor John Pentland, made about leadership in the church. "It is interesting how we have changed our leadership. We were taught empowerment and so we told people to just go ahead, do whatever you want to do. They looked at us and said, 'What am I supposed to do?' So our philosophy now would be more equipping the laity and teaching them to be ministers in their own right."

Ferguson and Pentland understand that enabling and equipping people for ministry and lived faith means more than just giving permission. Congregational members need to have form and framework to what they are called to do. Within the complexity of people who gather as the church, a participatory lifestyle by leaders is required to train and equip people. These leaders will champion the ministry involvement of congregational members, work alongside them, and resource them in the companionship of ministry.

The difference between controling and enabling appears to lie in the way clergy-leaders treat people.

Consistently, in our leadership interviews, clergy named their primary role as leaders to be enabling and equipping. "I really want to give them hope," said one leader. "I want to say something that will trigger them to understand that with God's help and by God's grace and strength they can make a difference in the world."

The 418 questionnaires completed for this research highlighted the enabling profile of Future Faith leaders. When the "most often" and "often" responses are combined, 93% of respondents said that the ministers who served their church enabled and equipped them to perform ministry. Of those 93%, over half (56%) said their leaders used this enabling philosophy of ministry "most often." Clearly an enabling framework for ministry is crucial for church health and vitality.

By contrast, when the "most often" and "often" responses are combined, only 12% of the participants stated that their leaders needed to be in control of everything (4% "most often"). This considerable difference between leaders who enable and those who control portrays the desire that congregational members feel to be partners in the life of the church. They respond to clergy-leaders who involve them into ministry. One focus group member referred to her minister's ability to "provoke or create an atmosphere" in which others get involved and excited about ministry and service.

The difference between controlling and enabling appears to lie in the way clergy-leaders treat people. If people feel like a number, like pawns moved around a chessboard at the will of the leader, then Canadian congregational members will resist.

FOCUSED ON GIFTS

The second question from the survey sheds even more light on the stark difference between a leadership style that enables and one that controls.[6]

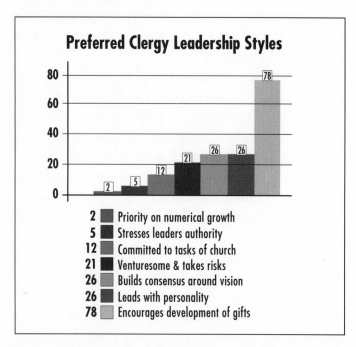

Preferred Clergy Leadership Styles

2 ■ Priority on numerical growth
5 ■ Stresses leaders authority
12 ■ Committed to tasks of church
21 ■ Venturesome & takes risks
26 ■ Builds consensus around vision
26 ■ Leads with personality
78 ■ Encourages development of gifts

Future Faith ministry development is gift focused. When asked how leaders help to create a healthy and effective church, 78% of the people replied that this occurred when clergy leadership encourage church members to discover and develop their gifts for service and ministry. Gift participation rises out of the passions and values people hold for a particular issue. Clearly, people in Future Faith churches feel worthwhile and are motivated to participate because they are working within their interests and abilities.

Leaders, to be effective, must adapt their leadership style to the person and context they are called to serve.

Paul Hershey and Kenneth Blanchard, writing from a business perspective, portray what enabling ministry looks like in Future Faith churches. They argue that effective leadership is a function of three variables:

- the leader
- the follower
- and the situation in which the leadership relationship occurs

Effective leaders understand these variables. They adapt their leadership to the people that they seek to influence in specific situations.

The crucial factor in this model is the maturity of both the leader and those being led. Maturity comes as participants develop confidence and competence in their ability to do the job. As that occurs, they are willing to accept more responsibility in seeing the task through to completion. Leaders, to be effective, must adapt their leadership style to the person and context they are called to serve. Leaders then focus on developing competence and confidence. They understand that there is more than one effective style of leadership, and are willing to adapt their style of leadership to the various maturity levels and people they are attempting to lead.

Hershey and Blanchard describe four basic styles that leaders employ to enable and empower people in different situations. These styles are defined by the amount of task direction that the leader provides and the amount of personal support and relational dependency that leaders encourage.

1. **Telling** style. This leadership style is very directive but maintains some relational distance. It is a style of enabling that is often used for new people who do not know how to do the job. They are not willing at the time to accept responsibility for the whole task because they lack competence or confidence. Telling leaders are highly directive as they encourage people to discover their potential.
2. **Selling** style. This style of leadership is more task directive but still provides relational support and encouragement. It provides needed direction but also engages in a relationship that reinforces confidence in a person.
3. **Participating** style. These leaders are highly supportive but non-directive. They provide strong encouragement but remain non-directive for those with a moderately high level of competence to complete the task but who lack the confidence to lead out on their own.
4. **Delegating** style. This style of leadership is non-directive and maintains a relational distance. It discourages dependence upon the leader because followers have the ability and the willingness to complete the task, proceeding with confidence on their own, effectively assuming leadership themselves.

Effective leaders will accept people where they are and adapt their leadership to produce growth and maturity. The goal in what is called "situational leadership" is to produce mature people within an organization – people who can lead on their own and develop maturity in others. The responsibility of leadership in the situational model is to move people from the lowest level of maturity (telling style) to the highest level (delegating style). A clergy leader described with excitement his joy in leading people to mature Future Faith living: "The adventure of ministry is that the people in the congregation begin to step out and minister; they begin to take responsibility for life, service, and servanthood."

PEOPLE OVER PROGRAMS

Unhealthy churches are often program-centered rather than people-centered. These churches put their hopes for life and growth in their structures and programs. As a result, their leaders spend an enormous amount of energy and time trying to fill programs with participants. In the process, they are often frustrated and disillusioned. Future Faith leaders, however, take a different focus. They seek the passions that people feel for particular issues and liberate them toward an opportunity to serve. Programs are not absent but they are filled with people energized about what they are doing.

This insight was stated by a focus group participant discussing his church. "We approach people and say, what is your passion? Where is an area that you would like to make an impact as you live your life? We identify that area and, if a program or an activity already exists, we follow them up. But if you have a new vision, and say this is my passion, we go for it. That is how you begin to impact your city with ministry."

Reflecting on this people orientation, Tim Dickau observes that in healthy churches people feel that they are cared about and valued. He explains, "We are a people. We're not about programs. If people have a sense that they're going to be here for each other, no matter what happens, then there's a feeling that 'I can cope.'"

Consulting, not Assigning

Our research affirms the findings in *Where's a Good Church?* where it was noted that "The prevailing mood in society at large also resides in the church. Unless leaders have created a private kingdom, people who think they can wield power by virtue of their position, or for that matter can exert personal power in order to reach their objectives, are simply out of touch."[7]

Future Faith leaders believe the church is a partnership. They are secure about their role as leaders in the church, but they invite others to share in the possibilities of ministry. A total of 42% of the people who filled out questionnaires believed that leaders who consult others are most effective. An overwhelming 86% indicated that their leaders used that style "most often" or "often."

As noted earlier, leaders who need to be in charge of everything were ineffective (4% identified control as the style their clergy employ). The pattern is consistent. Only 5% of the people in Future Faith churches said they would respond well to leaders who stressed authority based on position. And as few as 2% felt that a leader's emphasis on numerical growth would create a healthy and vibrant congregation.

Future Faith leaders work with people. Their ego strength allows for differences of opinion which do not hinder implementing a bigger vision of what they are called to do. They believe in a participatory leadership which works together with others in sharing the task. One focus group participant described this by saying, "The pastors don't do everything. They really encourage everyone in the church to be released to do what God has called them to do. That in turn allows us to be what we are called to be." Another participant added, "Lay ministry is important here. It is a very clear attitude that [our ministers] have and we all feel we are being ministers to one another." A leader agreed, "I think everyone has a ministry."

Sharing leadership and ministry does not mean opting out of responsibility. Congregational members perceive a clear distinction between leadership that consults (42%), delegates in a way which hands over leadership with built- in account-ability (35%), or simply assigns tasks (16%). Barry Parker, from St. John's Anglican, described the difference when he said that ministry is a sharing of lives where, as a leader, you need to acknowledge that "you are trying to work this out and you haven't got all the answers. God is doing a work in me. I am a father, I am a husband, a friend. I am trying to sort all this stuff out as well."

Consequently effective leaders don't self-image as people who have all the answers. They seek consensus and shared participation in the development of ministry and envision-ing a finer future. They do not simply assign tasks to people believing the work of ministry revolves around their per-sonal agendas.

The art of leadership can never be totally measured or fully described. But clearly, as we enter the next century, Future Faith leaders will be proactive and intentional about doing some things and avoiding others.

Effective leaders will

- **inspire** not **persuade**
- **enable** not **control**
- **consult** not **assign**.

LEADERS TAKE RISKS

Change is one certainty we can count on in the modern world. The unpredictable and tenuous nature of change will affect people in church congregations in different ways. We can also be certain that conflict, in the midst of and as a result of change, is inescapable as a church faces the future.

A mark of Future Faith leaders is that they have the capacity to manage conflict in healthy ways. Rather than avoiding conflict, they are ready to work through the issues of debate and seek successful conclusions. Carlin Weinhauer, pastor of Willingdon Church, the largest church in our research, knows what is worth fighting about and what is not. He told us, "We try to keep big things big and little things little, and ask God to show us which is which every day." This is not a simple feat in a 3000-plus member congregation. Strength and ability to manage change is directly related to how conflict is perceived. When some conflict is anticipated as an inevitable part of congregational life, no one is surprised, and resolutions can be found more easily.

Simply expecting conflict will not resolve conflict, though. There are risks in dealing with conflict in any situation. Some conflicts dissipate on their own. Others can escalate when they are addressed. But being ready to deal with conflict and the risk that it involves fits with the Future Faith leader profile of being venturesome.

The leaders we spoke with are willing to take risks and strike out in uncharted paths. With typical Canadian caution only 21% of the Future Faith respondents "strongly agreed" that leadership should take risks. However, when those who also "agree" are added to the response, 83% of the congregational members believed that the creation of spiritually alive and effective churches depends on leaders who are willing to be venturesome and take risks. An interpretation is merited: Future Faith churches are populated with people who are open to taking risks but not too enthusiastic about the prospects of risk taking!

Future Faith leaders believe the church is a partnership.

Future Faith church members signal a reluctance toward free-wheeling entrepreneurial leadership. This disposition seems to be built into the Canadian ethos. Still, it appears that church members acknowledge that taking some risk and being venturesome is a requirement for healthy congregational life. Leaders, similarly, understand that risk-taking initiatives create change, and that changes trigger inevitable conflict. Wise leaders therefore keep others involved in the process of strategy building and decision-making. As previously noted, 42% of the participants described their leaders as people who will consult others in the decision-making process.

A leader's ability to embrace change, and its inevitable partner conflict, is directly related to his or her personal sense of security. Leaders rooted in a personal identity which does not depend on their position will be liberated to serve in complex circumstances. The apostle Paul, an impressive leader in his time, constantly addresses the issue of identity. He roots ministry and service in the Christian image of being "in Christ." The foundation for a secure identity acknowledges that we are loved by Christ – whether the people around us love us or not. This rooted identity "in Christ" enables leaders to be free in their leadership role – including dealing with change and conflict. One Future Faith leader said it well: "My identity is constructed in a loving grace-filled relationship with Jesus Christ."

LEADERS LEAD, SO THEY CAN TRANSFORM

Again, the research results are decisive. Leaders are a crucial factor in the creation of healthy and vibrant congregational life. While the literature on leadership addresses this issue too, the participants in our research also underscore the need for clergy who see themselves as catalysts in motivating mission in the local church. As Charles Van Engen states, leadership is primarily a "missiological event" which is the product of the empowering activity of the Holy Spirit, the catalytic enabling of the leaders, and the serving work of the members.[8]

Leaders who face leadership tasks with reluctance produce passive churches. They hope for ministry and mission to take place through the local church without intentionally nurturing an atmosphere for soul care and social care to take root. Future Faith clergy are proactive. They believe that faith in Jesus Christ necessitates a "love God and love your neighbor" approach which must be intentionally fleshed out. They model what is possible and inspire people to achieve other possibilities. As Van Engen writes, "The spiritual, emotional and mental personhood of their leaders provides the *heart* of missionary congregations. Their managerial acumen provides the *structure* for missional outreach and the members provide the *hands, feet,* and *spiritual gifts* necessary to carry out the congregation's missional intentions."[9]

The shift from pastoral to missionary leadership underscores the difference between clergy as managers and clergy as leaders. In their book *Leaders*, Warren Bennis and Burt Nanus argue that many organizations, especially ineffective ones, are overmanaged and underled. Conversely, the common characteristic of effective leaders is their ability to *transform*. If leadership is crucial to the future life of the church, then the transformational focus of that leadership is imperative.

Clergy who opt out of the catalytic role create passive inward congregations. American church consultant Loren Mead goes so far as to state; "Clergy are a key resource for the future of the church. They are badly needed to ground the new structures in which lay people will gather to be formed and sent. They are critical training officers for the church of the future."[10] It is a prophetic call to a more proactive and mission oriented ministry framework that requires leaders who intentionally work as catalysts for change and mission development.

Transformational leaders create a common social responsibility. They stimulate people to "buy into" and to "own" a vision. They help participants to know what needs to be done and at the same time provide an atmosphere of joy to get on with the task. Transformative leaders free up and pool collective energies to pursue a common goal.[11] One Future Faith leader captured this transformational dimension by telling us, "The greatest satisfaction is seeing people get it, get faith and not religion. When people discover faith, God works."

During the research project, participants in the focus groups and respondents to the questionnaires confirmed the crucial role of leadership as catalysts who transform. The leaders embody the new orientation that will be required for churches in the future. While transcending style and personality, they view themselves as transformational forces in the congregation. They realize their role in the life of the church is critical. Presbyterian Terry Ingram embodies what we are saying: "I want to lead people to be the best God can make them to be. I want them to be receptive to what God is doing in their lives, and hopefully have the grace to back down and trust God's Spirit to do the rest."

Churches without transformational leaders are like the Tin Man in *The Wizard of Oz*. They have all the form but none of the heart for living. As a consequence they never produce the passion from which mission can take place. Future Faith leaders have a key role to play. Their effectiveness is measured by what they personally contribute, but more importantly, by how the people of God around them are equipped, enabled and inspired by the Spirit of God to participate in the mission of the church to the world.

5

ENERGIZING FUTURE FAITH CHURCHES

A church building without committed people and strong leaders is like a computer without software. It has shape and design but it just sits there dormant and lifeless. When you reach out and touch it, there is no response. Computers without software, like churches without dedicated people, only represent potential. Their promises crash in a heap of mere speculation.

Fortunately, there are people in churches across the land who have the spiritual software that helps them pursue their potential. They are fulfilling their intended purpose. People are touched by a loving God, and they reach out to others with the same love that touched them. Increasing numbers of people are active in these churches and their involvement deepens their personal faith.

These churches have their flaws, of course, but their energy and vision for what God is doing keeps them seeking a finer future. The Future Faith churches we have been describing are among the faith communities across the country that fit this description.

SPIRITUALLY ENERGIZED

While conducting leadership interviews and facilitating the focus groups, we soon realized that people in Future Faith churches are spiritually energized. God's spirit is in touch with their spirits. They communicate a sense of shared mission and vision. There is a commendable clarity about what the church is meant to be. And they value their churches. The thought of having to move and be forced to find another church is painful for them to consider.

MINISTRY MODELS, NOT PROTOTYPES

Beyond having strong convictions about the church's mission, Future Faith churches also have clearly defined ministry models. They know what is important to them. Their programs are purpose motivated. The activities of these churches fit within a framework.

Ministry models for churches are like major highways on a provincial map. The patterns are evident; the details have to be worked out on the ground. Like the highways, these ministry models are marked with signs that help lay people and their leaders know what direction to turn when they come to an intersection. Ministry models keep churches headed toward their destination. They let them know when they have slipped off the road and have begun traveling in the ditch. They provide reference points to let people know when they are lost and how to return to the desired direction.

Ministry models are not the same as church prototypes. Ministry models give churches a conceptual framework for determining their ministry emphases and programs strategies. In theological terms, churches with defined models exist with a clear ecclesiology. They have biblical convictions about the mandates for the people of God. Church prototypes, on the other hand, are usually high profile churches in some other place. These churches have developed reputations for being highly effective. They are marked with innovation, fast growth, and articulate leadership; they give evidence that God is doing a great work in their presence. Examples of current prototypes being

The patterns are evident; the details have to be worked out on the ground.

acclaimed are the Airport Christian Fellowship (formerly Vineyard) in Toronto, Willow Creek Community Church near Chicago, and Saddleback Community Church in Southern California. Significant numbers of leaders and their churches in Canada are attempting to transplant what is happening in prototype churches in other places.

Prototype churches tend to copy slavishly what has happened elsewhere. Ministry models, by contrast, allow a church to develop its own personality and style.

An analysis of the spiritual vitality in the Future Faith churches reveals a four dimensional ministry model. In remarkable ways, the people who worship and participate are spiritually energized. The implementation of the ministry model with its themes and emphases activates people. Clearly, life flourishes in people's hearts, minds, hands and voices. In their journeys with God and each other, they become more alive and more spiritually whole people. Specifically, the model generates:

- Affection for the **heart** through **worship**
- Insight for the **mind** through **learning**
- Behavior for the **hands** through **service**
- Meaning for the **voice** through **witness**

(See graphic on next page.)

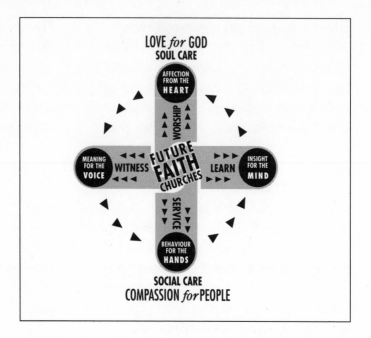

Affection for the Heart through Worship

The 418 people who responded to the survey from the 14 churches define themselves as "the committed". Their dedication translates into frequent church attendance. Around 90% attend at least once a week and virtually everyone at least once a month. Nine out of ten also claim to be formal members of their churches. When asked "How important to your faith is attending worship services?" 86% said it was "very important." And even more significantly, 88% agree that they "usually experience God's presence at a worship service."

WORSHIP WITH AFFECTION

Worship without affection is like black gospel music without rhythm, feeling, crescendo, or soul. Worship and sacred ritual without a response from the heart is like crying without tears. Future Faith churches, on the other hand, can be thought of as "inspiration centers." The centrality and importance of worship consistently crosses denominational lines and connects lay people and clergy with the presence of God.

Worshiping with affection is about opening your heart to celebrate who you are in Christ. It is welcoming the presence of God into the deepest level of your conscious and unconscious self. In worship, the soul is restored. In Future Faith congregations, people are invited to open themselves to the sacred. "My soul finds its rest in thee," say the words of a familiar hymn. Worshiping with affection from the heart allows people to release themselves to the God of creation who deserves their confidence and adoration.

A woman participant from the Christian Reformed Church described her experience: "On Sunday morning people are excited about their relationship with the Lord and you just want to celebrate." Pastor Carlin Weinhauer is enthusiastic about worship at Willingdon Community: "This place cooks on Sunday mornings, just cooks. There's an expectation. God is here. God is experienced here." The same refrain rings true for Wesley Campbell at the Vineyard Church in Kelowna: We experience God here. And that fuels all the rest of the stuff. "We experience God and we have hot worship and strong prayer meetings."

MUSIC FOR THE HEART

Music is another aspect of worship that feeds the heart and nourishes the soul. Just as the inner spirits of young people are stirred by the sounds of their favorite performers, people in Future Faith churches are emotionally affected and spiritually touched by the music in worship.

Many different kinds of music inspire people. A Catholic respondent spoke with feeling when he described part of the mass: "Father sings that preface and I just curl inside. It is so moving to hear him sing the words. I just can't express how it hits me." Of a different style of music, a Vineyard worshiper observed: "The children get involved in the dancing and the tambourines and the clapping and the joy of celebrating in worship. It's fun for the children to come to this place."

Listening to the experience of another participant reveals a striking contrast in style, but the significance of the music is the same. This is how a focus group participant explained what worship meant to her, "There is a 10-year-old girl who grins at me. She'll be in front of me or at the altar serving and turns around and grins when the 'Gloria' starts because she thinks it is so great that she can join in the singing. That's what feeds the people who are starving."

MOTIVATION FOR DIFFERENT LIVING

People sometimes wonder why worship issues can cause so much dissension and conflict in the church family. Resistance to change is often blamed. The deeper reason is that worship is the focal point from which congregational life flows. It is more than symbolic that worship is the most frequent function on the calendar of local church life. Worship stimulates congregations to encounter God and affects people personally.

When worship is right, it touches the heart but it also stimulates more than just emotional feelings. Worship motivates people into action. It prompts people in the pews to practice in their daily lives the truth they encounter in their worship services. In Future Faith churches, worship nurtures both soul care and social care in congregational life.

Evangelical futurist George Barna insists that churches must "shed existing attitudes of piety and solemness, in favor of attitudes of anticipation, joy and fulfillment."[1] While his market-oriented motives can be commended for their desire to reach the unchurched, Barna risks selling out to the present culture of happiness. Certainly, vital worship is about anticipation and joy. But unless worshipers alter their ways of living, the worship experience ends with the benediction. In a Catholic focus group the question was asked: "If you were to move and have to leave this church, what would you miss?" The response from a middle aged man was profound: "I would miss the quality of the liturgy. It inspires me to love and forgive."

Genuine worship is more than just a good feeling. Encountering God in worship motivates people to live differently.

CREATING SUPPORTIVE COMMUNITIES

Worship that touches the heart and motivates new levels of behavior also makes the creation of community possible. No other aspect of church life has such community-creating power. In turn, Christian community has the capacity to transcend diversity and unite varieties of people in supportive congregational life.

Clearly, participants in Future Faith churches are being nourished by their experiences of what the New Testament names as *koinonia.*

Supportive communities allow people to enter into church life at their own speed. As people are increasingly affected by the worship life of the congregation, they tend to become more involved. Yet one of the characteristics of supportive church communities is that people can be involved without feeling pressure to get more involved. A Presbyterian woman observed that although in her church there are so many possible activities to join that it's hard not to be involved, but "You never feel coerced or crowded to do something." A man from Grandview Calvary articulated the same message: "I felt welcomed but without pressure to perform. That's something I really value here."

Worship that affects the heart provides fertile ground for relationship building. The warmth of Christian fellowship draws people together and gives them a sense of belonging. Friendships flourish; when people are absent, it is noticed. With a twinkle in his eye, Dan Doolittle revealed: "When our people come into the church, they are always hugging one another. That's why I call them 'care bears.'"

Participants repeatedly talked about being able to sit and talk to other people who are having similar struggles. They value being able to wrestle with the same questions or burdens. Quality relationships in supportive faith communities often lead to measures of mutual accountability. A member of the Mennonite Brethren church appreciated that his community encourages members to lean on each other and to experience how being vulnerable with each other is helpful. The consequence? "We are starting to feel Christianity as opposed to just having it be a head thing."

A Catholic participant summarized some of the main merits of worshiping in a healthy Christian community: "We deal with one another as we are, not as we ought to be or as we should be. For me, that's one of the fundamentally important things of any Christian community. I find that here." Supportive faith communities release people to be their true selves. And in those environments people can grow and develop confidence in themselves as well as in the God who created them.

Supportive communities allow people to enter into church life at their own speed.

Members of the clergy made similar statements to those expressed by lay people. Doug Ward from Kanata Baptist finds personal freedom in his church environment: "I can be myself here and I feel very strongly most other people can too." Presbyterian Terry Ingram unashamedly declared, "I'm just happy when I plunk myself down in the midst of humanity here." Wesley Campbell from the Vineyard church offered his view: "We're building the family of God here ... People get set free from their garbage, they get encouraged and they find friends to walk beside them."

David Watt knows that soul care worship is at the center of Future Faith communities. When he was asked the question: "Five years from now, if you were not here, what would disappoint you?" he replied, "If we lost the sense of God's presence, I mean if our worship was empty – that would disappoint me. If people didn't say I'm really glad that I came here because I found God here and I found a sense of community and acceptance here – that would disappoint me."

In addition to being nurturing supportive human communities, Future Faith churches help people experience the presence of God. The combination is spiritually potent.

Early in his ministry, Jesus came back home to Nazareth and preached a sermon at the synagogue where he had worshiped as a youth. He began by declaring: "The Spirit of the Lord is upon me, because he has anointed me ... (Luke 4:18). Jesus had been touched by the spirit of his father in heaven. His human spirit was aware of an indwelling divine spirit. The presence of God was in him.

The same divine spirit that brought life to Jesus continues to bring spiritual life to people in Future Faith churches and other churches too. God's alive people are injected with the presence of the resurrected Christ. They are people who have been touched by God. In worship they experience the presence of the divine and affection flows from their hearts to God. When they are wounded and broken, they turn to the Great Physician for healing. God's people know what it is to find rest for their souls.

Jesus' sermon that Sabbath morning didn't stop with his declaration of being spirit anointed. He went on to describe his mission to the poor and oppressed. As well as bringing good news to the poor, Jesus said he had been sent to proclaim release to the captives and recovery of sight to the blind, to let the oppressed go free. (Luke 4:18 NRSV). Human hearts that have been touched by God are also energized to join Jesus in his mission. People are motivated to live differently. In tangible ways, they care for people who are captives of circumstances, in situations that rob their freedom and the ability to fully care for themselves.

More than simply believing that God exists, Future Faith people experience that God is real. They sense they are loved by the creator and redeemer of the universe and their love reaches back to God and people around them. As individuals and in their faith communities, their hearts are warmed and spiritually energized.

Insight for the Mind through Learning

But there is more to a lively and vibrant faith than just receiving spiritual heart massages. As important as worship is in stirring affection for the heart, the head also needs some attention.

In the case of Future Faith churches, that additional need is met by offering insight for the mind. And as with worship, the disposition and expectation to learn crosses denominational lines. At the Chinese Baptist Church we heard, "A very important ministry is to educate people." A United Church participant spoke with appreciation for spiritual understanding: "I would say one of the biggest changes for me has been the depth of learning about my spirituality."

LEARNING WITH A SPIRIT OF GRACIOUS ORTHODOXY
There are variances, but the overall tone of truth expressed in Future Faith churches is marked with gracious orthodoxy. Christian conviction is communicated with clarity but without the exclusiveness often attributed to fundamentalism. A Baptist voice is representative of others: "We don't just hear opinions from the pulpit. What we hear is, 'This is God speaking. It's not just me. I've considered it carefully and this is what I believe God says.'"

SHARING A COMMON CONVICTION
Voices from other denominations echo similar commitments. Without being overly simplistic, the Christian faith is assumed to be based on truth and both the Scriptures and Jesus Christ are affirmed as trustworthy reference points for the faithful. Consider the following perspectives:

- Presbyterian: *The word of God is held up as truth. It's not subject to a whole lot of amorphous kinds of interpretation or subjective preview to support what feels good. There is openness somehow, but there is unity at the same time in the right things.*

- Chinese: *The one basic thing our church is based on is who is Jesus Christ. From there on we talk about sacrificing ourselves, following the Lord and maturing in the Lord.*
- Anglican: *We learn from the Bible and we know that sin is wrong, but we also know that everyone does sin. We don't have fire and brimstone sermons. Our ministers preach on the positive, but we know that sin is disappointing to God.*

Future Faith Christians know what is important to believe. Their well-established Christian convictions are like living with a healthy backbone. Without being fully conscious of the strength they bring, they are simply present.

The perspectives voiced in the focus groups are confirmed by the research data. Future Faith church people embrace the Christian essentials. The Scriptures are believed to be reliable. Truth becomes a reference point for determining what is right and what is wrong.

Future Faith people are also church people. Compared to other representative Canadians who also attend church weekly, the Future Faith people believe attendance is more mandatory. They are also more inclined to accept the church's teaching. Overall, people in Future Faith churches are more conservative in their religious beliefs than other regular attenders in the Canadian church population.

	PERSONAL BELIEFS		
	% agreeing		
	Future Faith Churches	Canada Wkly. Attenders	Canada General Pop.
I believe the Bible to be the inspired word of God	99	92	65
Truth is important to me	80	n/a	n/a
I consider myself to be a converted Christian	76	72	35
My private beliefs about Christianity are more important than what is taught by any church	34	72	63
I don't think you need to go to church to be a good Christian	31	54	92
What is right and wrong is a matter of personal opinion	14	49	56

Source of data:
Future Faith Churches: World Vision Canada: Nov. 1996; N: 415
Canada Weekly Attenders: Angus Reid Group/PEW: 1996; N: 619
Canada General Population: Angus Reid Group: 1994 & 1996; N: 3000

Affirming Christian orthodoxy is crucial to maintaining a clear Christian commitment. However, if right belief is all that there is to being Christian, then faith will be reduced to personal piety. A lay participant linked belief with practice when she said, "If we don't have sound teaching first, then we won't have the good works after."

APPLYING PERSONAL DISCRETION

Another facet of learning with a spirit of gracious orthodoxy in Future Faith churches is that Christian conviction is complemented with Christian discretion. On the one hand, they readily embrace the basic beliefs of the faith. But on the other hand, they reserve the prerogative to personally interpret the meaning of those beliefs. Legalism would feel like an outsider in the pews of Future Faith churches.

In Future Faith churches, instead of clergy decreeing what Christians ought to do, lay people are granted room to determine what is right and best in the sight of God. Corbin Eddy from Saint Basil's Catholic church articulated the attitude of most of the Future Faith clergy: "I can't tell people how to live their lives. What I can do is invite people to recognize their membership in Christ. I can invite them to recognize the spirit that's at work in their lives." Barry Parker from St. Johns Anglican shared a similar perspective: "To tell people how to live is dumb. Instead, I say 'Here's what God says about how to live. Now, what are you going to do about it?'"

A further example of Christian discretion was expressed by a Presbyterian participant: "Our minister gives you more than one point of view and then he leaves you to think about it. He doesn't just give you his answer at the end, which is great."

It was enlightening to listen to people compare their personal histories with their present faith journeys. A man who attends The Meeting Place reflected on his experience: "Growing up in the church, I knew that there was a list of do's and don'ts. As a good Mennonite Christian, I don't dance and I don't smoke and I don't drink, and I don't have premarital sex. What I feel is happening at the Meeting Place is that people are saying we're on the journey of trying to learn how to live as followers of Christ."

REACHING OUT WITH COMPASSION
Holding to the belief that Jesus Christ is central has ramifications for how God's people view others – especially those who

don't think of Jesus as important. When one believes the Bible is reliable and that Jesus is for them "the way, the truth and the life," one wishes others should believe likewise. In the case of "feeling it is important for non-Christians to become Christians," eight out of ten Future Faith people are in agreement. They are decidedly more evangelistic in their spirits than other weekly attenders in the nation.

Future Faith churches excel at allowing people to find something solid to grab onto or something more flexible to lean against.

On the question of "all the great religions of the world being equally good and true," Future Faith people are again significantly more conservative than other regular attenders.

ATTITUDES TOWARD THE BELIEFS OF OTHERS			
% agreeing			
	Future Faith Churches	Canada Wkly. Attenders	Canada General Pop.
I feel it is important to encourage non-Christians to become Christians	82	60	26
Christianity is only one route to salvation	40	n/a	n/a
All the great religions of the world are equally good and true	18	56	67

Source of data: as in page 133

Considering the orthodox nature of their personal beliefs, their conservative stand on world religions, and their desire for others to become Christians, it seems inconsistent that four out of ten believe that "Christianity is only one route to salvation." Acknowledging a range of differences among the 14 surveyed churches, how can we explain the apparent contradiction?

Future Faith people are neither judgers nor dissenters. They are followers of Jesus marked with compassion. Remember, they belong to communities of grace. Accepting people is their manifesto. Absence of judgment characterizes their churches. The predisposition of Future Faith people is simultaneously to affirm the validity of their own faith while both responding to God and caring for others. Rather than investing their energy in thinking "we are right and others who don't agree with us are wrong," they are people finding their way on their own spiritual journeys.

When Jesus was on earth, he self-imaged as a physician. Jesus said, "Those who are well have no need of a physician, but those who are sick; I have come ... (Luke 5:31) In line with that text, Harold Percy from Streetsville Anglican images the church as a hospital. He claims: "It's a place to heal. Hospitals don't tell people to go home because they're sick."

In a similar way, Jennifer Ferguson, minister at Deer Park United in Calgary, sees the church as a healing center for the wounded. She says this role is important because people "have to be healed to serve."

The combination of accepting people and having a vision for their healing complements the spiritual orientation of Future Faith churches that focuses on the positive side of the gospel. Judging others, including people from other world faiths, is simply not the Future Faith way. The insight and confessional spirit of a Catholic participant is illustrative: "To preach the gospel is to show the joy of what 'thou shalt,' rather than what 'thou shall not.'" Future Faith people are more predisposed to affirm the positive than to accentuate the negative. That attitude extends to others, whether or not they share a common faith.

The hallmarks of Christian learning are gracious orthodoxy buoyed by conviction and compassion. Future Faith churches excel at allowing people to find something solid to grab onto or something more flexible to lean against. These churches do the soul care of preparing people to accept themselves before God so that these same individuals can help others in the name of God.

LEARNING THE BASICS OF FAITH

Do not equate the commitment of Future Faith churches to understand the faith more deeply with enrolling in seminary to complete a theological degree. The approach is more linked to being an adult lifelong learner.

Although some Future Faith churches have a core curriculum that they offer to their people, their greater concern is to first establish people in the basics of the Christian faith. Without demeaning anyone, these churches operate with (in varying degrees) two assumptions:

- Churched and unchurched people are religiously illiterate
- People are open to learn.

The experience of one Anglican individual is illustrative, "The aim here is to teach people. Not everybody comes from the same background. Not everybody was awake during communion classes."

Learning environments are nurtured. Churches that live with closed systems are more inclined to dispense answers and to indoctrinate their people than they are to create environments with the freedom to ask questions. Churches with more open systems, on the other hand, systems that envision their people on spiritual journeys, are more apt to hear their members say things like, "I've grown up in this church and I've had questions and I feel very open about asking those questions." People who ask questions that trouble their spiritual well-being are on the road to mature and healthy faith commitments.

Corbin Eddy from Saint Basil's is a teacher who intentionally nurtures a learning environment by arousing his parishioner's imaginations. Eddy says that his motivation is to spark religious imagination so that people realize that most of our limitations are really a lack of experience.

Understanding the current deficits of religious knowledge and need for a better understanding of the faith, Presbyterian Terry Ingram confesses that he has "a continued long-range goal to increase biblical literacy. We need to know the story. We need to know why we are what we are."

LEARNING IN SMALL GROUPS

One of the primary forums for learning in Future Faith churches is small groups. Overall, one half of those in the Future Faith survey participated weekly in a small group that involves Bible study, prayer, or some expression of community service. In the case of the Willingdon Community Church, they theme their small groups as discovery classes.

The small group experience is multi-dimensional. Although some form of Bible study, prayer and discussion is central to most groups, measures of accountability, discipleship, and pastoral care also occur. A Vineyard participant saw the small group as "where our growth is encouraged and where we learn to walk on our spiritual legs." A woman from the Christian Reformed church spoke in a similar manner: "I love the public teaching, but I find when you apply it to daily life, it's more of a struggle than a eureka. The small group is where you can struggle with your faith and say what you do in your workplace."

Future Faith churches and their people are in touch with the times.

Small groups are not for everyone. Even in the Future Faith churches where small group involvement is available for almost everyone, approximately half of the people do not participate. Still, the small groups are crucial to the whole church. They are places where people go deeper in their faith. Sometimes they play a role in a church's outreach. A Mennonite Brethren parishioner whose first contact with the church was through a small group explained that "the group brings smallness to a big church."

Clearly, small groups are places where God's people experience both relationships and community. In the focus groups, a repeated refrain was "You still have a big church with the fellowship and the worship, but the little group is the nitty-gritty place where you can get help and give help."

LEARNING FOR LIVING IN COMPLEXITY

Churches are often criticized by secular forces for pulling people out of the world rather than equipping them to live in the world. The assumption is that Christians gather in worship, study in small groups, and program themselves into a subculture. Certainly, some churches specialize in separating and protecting their people from the ways of the world.

This is not the case with Future Faith churches. Their pattern is more consistent with the findings of the *Where's a Good Church* study conducted in 1993.[2] The research in that study established that, rather than pulling people out of the world, effective churches emphasize the relevance of the faith by giving attention to the circumstances in the world. Like other effective churches, Future Faith churches and their people are in touch with the times.

The Christian Reformed Church has a long tradition of integrating faith with all of life. In the focus group, the conviction that faith and life are connected was expressed eloquently: "God has an understanding and an ability to show love through my family life, my work life, my friendship life, economic life. Whatever it is, God speaks to that."

A similar view was articulated in the Chinese Baptist church: "We can apply our faith to our struggles at home and at work and at school. We can turn them into something positive." The same emphasis was voiced at The Meeting Place: "Application is the emphasis – what is the relevance of Christianity in terms of how you live your life."

In the survey of Future Faith church attenders, there were high levels of satisfaction around specific issues that challenge our thinking and living.

IS YOUR CHURCH GIVING ADEQUATE DIRECTION IN THESE AREAS?	
	% saying yes
People's personal spiritual needs	93
Making moral decisions in today's society	89
Practical ways to respond to community needs	87
Problems of family life	85
Living as a Christian in the workplace	85
Social problems facing our country today	73

Future Faith people are learning to live in the complexity of today's world. Clergy are striving to teach with relevance, and lay people are making the connections. A statement made in the Catholic context reflects what is occurring elsewhere: "For me what is important is that the homilies are grounded in today as well as being grounded in scripture."

Paul Wilkie, a lay person concerned about following Jesus in these times, reinforces the cry of God's people when he says, "We need

A set of principles we can take into the bedroom as well as the boardroom.

a Jesus in the home, on the street, on the job, in the community and world – as well as a Jesus in church or private prayer. We need a Jesus who is consistent, and yet able – and who can help *us* to be able – to deal with the inconsistencies and ever-changing circumstances of life."[3]

LEARNING FOR SERVING

Future Faith people are learning to connect their worship with their work and their personal experiences of divine presence with the demands of modern life. Studying the Bible together is one source that provides direction. Again, reflecting on his small group experience, one Anglican member stated, "When you follow the Bible's teaching you develop a value system that sets patterns for your every- day life." Contrasting learning for living with knowing theology, a Christian Reformed parishioner explained: "Instead of walking out and knowing a whole bunch of theology, you know how to apply it to your daily life. I mean everybody can say 'Okay, I live a good Christian life,' but what we thought was okay at one point in our walk we now look at in a more mature way. When you see how you were wrong – you grow."

One encouraging pattern in the Future Faith churches is that study and learning is not an end in itself. Solid theory leads to coherent practice. For a Mennonite Brethren participant, the small group is where ministry and serving occurs often: "If somebody loses a job, that gets looked after by those in the Bible study small group. If there's a sickness in the family, they're visited in the hospital. If somebody dies, the care of that family comes through members of the group."

The response to need and pastoral care also extends to others outside the church. A Baptist articulated what most other Future Faith churches would affirm: "When the individual people who choose to make this their church home intersect with the community in 101 different ways on any given day, that's most important."

There is a yearning from the inside, a deep longing in the soul of Paul Wilkie as he pleads for an adequate faith in these times:

What we seek is a belief at once transcendently compelling and eminently practical – a true, reliable, and lasting light to illuminate our lives; a spiritual force to infuse our beings and inform our judgments; a compass by which to set our course. We want something to help us live life and confront death, a way to shape our morality, a set of principles we can take into the bedroom as well as the boardroom – a faith that can weather our various trials, moods, and seasons. We yearn for a life rooted in, but not stunted by, religious tradition – a value structure that can wisely assay the worth and role of secular culture, yet preserve us from being enslaved by it.[4]

A faith such as this can only flow from the combination of a divinely energized heart and a fully awakened mind. This section on "insight for the mind through learning" began with the emphasis on how a spirit of gracious othodoxy helps us to "learn the basics." There is nothing more basic, more biblical and more fundamental to the Christian faith than Jesus' validation of the

Great Command. The call is clear. Without neglecting other dimensions of human life, "love God with your mind."

Behavior for the Hands through Service

Energized hearts and awakened minds cannot be contained. Indifference to neighbors in need is not an option when God is rooted in the inner spirits of transformed people and the truth of the gospel is embedded in the minds of the followers of Jesus. Compassion is translated into action; visions for mercy ministries emerge. The theory of the gospel is authenticated in the lives of God's people reaching out and caring for others.

Future Faith churches are a part of this combination of divine-human activity. With their time and energy, with their helping hands and compassionate spirits, they are loving their neighbors. Without projecting a social utopia or sending out news releases to the media, they are demonstration centers of the love of God and compassion of Christ.

The following list of community ministries was compiled from references made by participants in the focus groups and the clergy leadership interviews. The list is more representative than exhaustive. Had we requested the 14 churches to submit a full list of all their community ministry commitments, it would be longer.

- Youth drop in centers
- Food banks
- Programs for senior citizens
- Prison ministries
- Camp programs
- Parenting skills classes

- Twelve step programs
- Street shelters
- Soup kitchens
- Cooking classes
- Habitat for humanity projects
- Service mission trips
- Refugee sponsorships
- Telecare – a congregational check-up program
- Facilities in support of AA meetings
- Single parent support programs
- Crisis pregnancy centers
- Programs for youth
- Counseling centers
- English as a second language
- Tutoring
- Housing units for low income families
- AIDS hospice
- 30 hour famine
- NeighbourLink
- Low interest community development loans
- Personal emergency loans
- Small business development assistance

At both church organizational levels and in their personal lives, Future Faith Christians affirm the gospel's call to love their neighbors in practical ways. In the survey, 8 of 10 participants said that it was very important for their church "to serve people in their communities who have needs." The same number claimed that in their personal faith it is very important "to respond to people's needs in my community."

In attitude and practice, the patterns of Future Faith churches are the fulfillment of what 1960s prophet Francis

Schaeffer believed about the church: "Unless people see in our churches not only the preaching of the truth but the practice of truth, the practice of love and the practices of beauty; unless they see ... faith being practiced in our communities, then let me say it clearly: They will not listen, and they should not listen."[5] Future Faith churches are practicing, and people are listening.

SERVING WITH HUMAN COMPASSION

The baseline for Future Faith Christians starts with the goodness of human compassion. The attitude articulated by a Chinese Church participant is an example: "You see people with specific problems or needs. They come to the church for help. They're not Christians. They have no intention to come to the church or to become Christian. They just have needs. People are willing to help, whether they're going to come to church or not."

The same spirit exists in other Future Faith churches. As one participant explained: "There's a real encouragement towards service. Nobody sits back. I mean, there's lots of volunteers. The right people come together." The orientation to respond to people's needs is structured into the formal structures of almost all Future Faith churches. The commitment to care in practical ways is transmitted beyond church structures to people in the pews.

A readiness to get involved is grounded in the inner attitudes and values of many of God's people as well as other Canadians who do not attend church. However, when Future Faith church attenders are compared to other weekly attenders in the nation or to those Canadians who do not attend church at all, Future Faith people reveal higher levels of social compassion. Whether the issue is getting churches

and other charities to help the poor, paying higher taxes so
the government can invest more in poverty concerns, or personally getting involved in responding to the needs of the poor
– Future Faith people lead the way.

COMPASSION FOR CANADA'S POOR			
% agreeing			
	Future Faith Churches	Canada Wkly. Attenders	Canada General Pop.
Because of government cutbacks, I feel there is the need for charities and other groups to help the poor and needy in our society	95	87	89
Churches and religious organizations should spend more money on helping the poor	83	80	84
The gap between the rich and poor in this country is a significant problem	76	75	77
The government should spend more to fight hunger and poverty even if it means higher taxes	61	56	60
Most people are poor because they don't work hard enough to get ahead in the world	8	21	20
It is best not to get too involved in taking care of other people's needs	4	19	22

Source of data: as in page 133

The pattern of being more compassionate than other Canadians also prevails when compassion toward global concerns
are examined. Even though Future Faith church attenders

have the same opportunities as other Canadians to be exposed to circumstances affecting others around the world, they are more ready to empathize with world needs. With predictability, when Future Faith church attenders are compared to other Canadians, they distinguish themselves as the most compassionate.

The omnipresence of television has helped create a borderless world. When we dial 1-800 numbers we have no idea where the person on the other end of the line is geographically located. With a computer and a modem we can have world wide access to other people's ideas and instant information on almost any subject. We can send and receive e-mail from almost any country in the world for mere pennies. Whenever there is a natural disaster in Bangladesh, a war in Africa, a famine in North Korea, political change in England, or a Bre-X fraud in Indonesia, we see and hear and know about what is happening. But how much does this rampaging globalization nurture a disposition to act with compassion toward those who live with little or no control over the circumstances that can victimize them?

COMPASSION FOR THE WORLD'S POOR			
% agreeing			
	Future Faith Churches	Canada Wkly. Attenders	Canada General Pop.
I feel I personally have an important responsibility to help people in poor countries around the world	83	74	60
Even in these difficult economic times government should maintain its current levels of aid to developing countries in the Third World	87	60	52

	Future Faith Churches	Canada Wkly. Attenders	Canada General Pop.
The number of immigrants who can legally enter Canada should be reduced	22	53	55

Source of data: as in page 133

Future Faith people live with extended arms toward others. They tend to be more inclusive and ready to see life from other people's point of view. Whether others come from Third World developing nations or from outside their faith communities, Future Faith people are ready to accept them and respond. When one's view of people includes the capacity and desire to care for others, doors of service get opened. David Watt from Dartmouth Baptist tells about his involvement in preparing for a service mission trip to Brazil. He heard an older man remark: "I want to help somebody, you know, I live in a nice home, I've got a good job, my wife's got a good job, I want to help somebody." Pastor Watt went on to exclaim: "So you give people that opportunity."

SERVING WITH DIVINE MOTIVATION

The virtue of compassion for others is not the only reason Future Faith churches respond to the needs of people. Barry Parker from St. Johns Anglican links the good desire to serve with divine motivation. Expressing a concern for the environment, he observes: "We trash the world around us and the creatures in it. God has created the world and the creatures in it. We're charged with the responsibility of looking after that. I'm God's steward of that, so I had better take care of it."

The focus group at Saint Basil's Catholic Church observed that "Faith means nothing unless it's transmitted into action. That's the message we get continuously. And that in turn sends people out to do the various things they do." Dan Doolittle from First Nations Pentecostal offered a spiritual motivation for action: "We always sing that song 'To be like Jesus.' The Scriptures say 'even as you do it unto the least of these you've done it unto me.' For too many years Native people have talked about

In most Canadian churches, the attenders are either middle class and white, or members of the same ethnic group.

their love for God, and I think it's time we walked it." A Baptist expressed similar sentiments: "Serving is your primary way of worshiping Christ."

People in Future Faith churches are being taught to serve, and they are doing so with divine motivation.

In the Vineyard Church there is an emphasis on freeing people to minister. Pastors don't do everything: "They really encourage everyone in the church to be released to do what God has called them to do. And that in turn allows us to be what we're called to be and to show who we are in Christ to others." Similarly, at The Meeting Place, the key is to free up people to serve. Said a person involved in ministry, "It's a matter then of discerning together, of coming alongside and saying how can we help make what God's put in your heart really happen."

When the Christian life is as it should be, God's spiritually hungry people take the bread and lift the cup, and out of a spirit of gratefulness they feed the hungry. They treat other people the way God treats them.

SERVING WITH COMMUNITY CONCERN

"This church cares about our community. It's not a big congregational clique," explained a woman from Kanata Baptist. Reflecting an obvious concern for her community, a woman from Grandview Calvary observed: "I think one of the most crucial things that's happened here is that we've asked the community, 'How do you see the church serving you?'"

Future Faith churches are more than just buildings located on plots of ground in geographical communities. They actively relate and respond to the concerns of the people who share those communities with them. And they do so with a generous spirit. Dan Doolittle offered a Native perspective on his community: "In the same way that Jesus broke fish and fed everybody who was there, God is a God of supply. In our native culture when the hunter used to go out and bring something back, it was shared with everybody. That's still part of our culture. When we have an abundance of food that God has blessed us with – our belief is to share it."

One indicator of healthy churches is that people from the surrounding community feel free to come inside the church, while active members see themselves dispersed into society as God's representatives. In Deer Park United, "People from the community come here. They are getting to the point that if they've got a problem and need some money to tide them over or if they have circumstances that have been nasty situations – they come and we can help them."

Vineyard churches have reputations for being both charismatic in style and encouraging signs and wonders. Kelowna Vineyard's pastor Wesley Campbell explained, "While we pray for revival, we do not neglect mercy in our own town." In yet another expressing concern for the community, a Baptist woman reflected on her personal experience: "Life is just like it was when I was on a mission field. I used to eat, sleep and work there, and basically I do the same here."

SERVING IN MULTI-ETHNIC COMMUNITIES

In 1971, when Parliament passed the Multicultural Act, Canada was officially designated a multicultural society. The Act affirms the racial diversity of Canadian society and seeks to create a more integrated culture. Regrettably, a true sense of social equality still eludes many Canadians. Whether it is immigration on the west coast, a legacy of judgmental memories on the east coast, or the emergence of enclaves of visible minorities in our major cities racist-like attitudes prevail too often in the nation. Many churches reflect this cultural isolation. In most Canadian churches, the attenders are either middle class and white, or members of the same ethnic group.

In this milieu, a number of Future Faith churches are intentionally working at integrating ethnic diversity into their faith communities.

Every church has a unique story to tell on who has been and who will be a part of their community. Acknowledging the Dutch roots in the Christian Reformed Church, Mike Rietsma affirms their attempt to be more inclusive. He says, "Our background is Dutch, but my first prayer when I came here was that we would be able to get beyond that ethnicity."

The Kanata Baptist church faced other circumstances. Doug Ward explains, "About four years ago we had a group of people from the Caribbean in our church. It just seemed to happen and their needs weren't being met. We intentionally got those people together and carefully identified their concerns. Out of that came a conference about multi-ethnic ministry. We brought in a specialist who had spent time in the

Philippines. We talked openly about what it means to be with people you don't know very well, about their backgrounds, about telling their stories."

Willingdon Community is a large church by Canadian standards. They have responded to the language diversity in their congregation. Carlin Weinhauer is pleased that they have been doing "simultaneous translation for eight years now in Korean." Recently, they added Russian, Japanese, Cantonese and Mandarin. Says Weinhauer, "One of our strong commitments is that the church needs to reflect the mix in the community. We will not allow people to say 'us and them.'"

Dan Doolittle captures the spirit of others. He astutely observes: "I've always encouraged people to go back to Genesis. We're *all* boat people. We all got off the same boat. Through Noah we all came from the same blood line. God doesn't see any differences in us. We may have different color skin, but we don't need racial barriers or any other barriers between us."

Although he was not focusing on multicultural issues, Francis Schaeffer eloquently expressed a fundamental truth about ministry: "We may preach truth, we may preach orthodoxy. We may even stand against the practice of untruth strongly. But if others cannot see something beautiful in our human relationships ... then we are not living properly."[6]

When social care initiatives reach out to the community, they not only respond to people's immediate needs, they also address issues like lurking racism and begin to restore a more just society. The spirit of Future Faith churches captures author Walter Burghardt's concerns, "As for the Jewish people, so for us: Not to execute justice is not to worship God."[7]

There was a time in Canada when the church was at the center of the community. Future Faith churches are demonstrating again that they can be spiritual centers in their communities – centers of both soul care and social care.

Meaning for the Voice through Witness

When the importance of "loving God and loving your neighbor as yourself" is lifted up for examination, Future Faith church people vote enthusiastically for both sides of the gospel equation. Whether you ask lay people or clergy, they believe firmly in faith that is profoundly personal and have difficulty conceiving the Christian life if it doesn't include deliberate caring for people who have needs.

Sacramental churches have long envisioned the work of God happening in lives of their parishioners when "The Lord's people gather around the Lord's table on the Lord's day." John Shea's apt description of church life reinforces the manner and method, "Gather the folks, tell the stories, break the bread."[8]

Mainline Protestant churches have traditionally functioned with a Christendom mindset. They have expected people who are born into Anglican, United, Presbyterian, or Lutheran families to simply "come to" church. Historically, parishes, synods, and presbyteries were geographically plotted across the country; it was assumed that people who lived inside the boundaries would show up inside their churches. Worship, rites of passage, confirmation, biblical teaching and other involvement in the family of faith would engender personal commitment and corporate spiritual vitality.

If mainline Protestants relied primarily on a "come to" strategy, evangelical Protestants added a "go to" strategy. Because they arrived later on the Canadian scene, evangelicals lacked a significant population segment who already identified themselves as fellow evangelicals. Evangelical Protestants have always needed an outreach orientation. With the exception of Baptists in the Maritime provinces, evangelical churches have been motivated to win a following of people who were born with connections to either mainline or Catholic traditions. As a result, they have been more proactive in their orientation to reach out. The evangelical focus on the "Great Commission" fueled their desire to reach the world and win people to Christ. In practice their church growth method was "go to" in order to "bring in." One of the distinctive differences that has helped to build evangelical churches has been to call people to make a clear decision for Christ and then to nurture the conversion experience through the ministry of the church.

Often labeled as a mainline evangelical church, Streetsville Anglican is effectively implementing a hybrid of the "come to – go to" approaches. To nurture Christian commitment and orchestrate church life, they have a threefold emphasis. During the focus group at Streetsville, most participants were able to recite: "Come in – Grow up – Go out."

Although different churches use diverse methods in their pursuit of Christian witness, Future Faith churches show remarkable agreement about the importance of outreach and evangelism. For example, eight out of ten members believe it is very important to "prepare for my Christian witness in the world and learn how to think about issues in a distinct Christian way". In the survey, there was equal support from Future Faith people for their church to emphasize "outreach to others" and "witnessing with words – while six out of ten claimed they "talk to others who do not attend church about spiritual matters" once a month or more. Future Faith people are finding Christian meaning for their voices.

When somebody shares their story with me, I feel like I'm on holy ground.

SPIRITUAL STORY TELLING

Whatever the circumstances that bring people into Future Faith churches, once they are inside, they hear the gospel story and share their spiritual stories with each other. Pastor Dickau from Grandview Calvary explains his strategy: "The Scriptures tell the story of God's hope for our lives ... I very much believe that as people grapple with that story it's going to change them too."

An example of the impact of one of the biblical stories was shared by a United Church parishioner: "Something that has really impacted me, is the biblical story of the burning bush – taking off your shoes because you're on holy ground. Now when somebody shares their story with me, I feel like I'm on holy ground. It has completely changed the way that I look at other human beings."

TELLING SPIRITUAL STORIES INSIDE

The role of story is multi-layered. There are God's series of stories communicated in the Scriptures. Then, there is God's story in our stories. And these stories are told both inside the church and beyond its walls, where the storytellers relate to others who may not know God's story.

A Catholic man in a focus group identified spiritual story telling as "a very powerful homiletic technique. It's something we've started to do as a community. We tell our spiritual stories, the good news stories. Issues take on a very different slant when you put a name and face and it's your grandson whose story comes to mind or your nephew, your granddaughter, or your mother." Kanata Baptist's Doug Ward contends that "in order to grow spiritually you need to be talking about your faith." In the Aboriginal Pentecostal church, "There's a lot of testimony in the congregation. That's very important because what you may be saying the Lord has done for you, somebody may be waiting for confirmation for themselves."

Excitedly, a woman from The Meeting Place offered both a testimony and an endorsement: "When you come here you can talk to anybody about Jesus. You can talk to them about what you're experiencing, what you are reading, the truth you are thinking about and everybody loves to hear it." During our leadership interviews, Paul Wartman explained the strategic design in spiritual story telling that happens at The Meeting Place: "Once you've shared your story at a believer's service and there's evidence of integrity and authenticity in your life, we invite some people to tell their stories again at one of our weekend services that are targeted towards seekers. What happens here on a Sunday morning serves to help that person share their faith in a relevant way."

TELLING THE STORIES OUTSIDE

Telling one's spiritual story to seekers in relevant ways inside the church is good practice for sharing the story outside the church walls. When people are given a context, a safe place to communicate what is happening between God and themselves, witnessing becomes more natural, more feasible. And those who listen gain confidence too. As one participant expressed it: "When I hear others talk about their walk with God, I think more deeply about my own."

Listening and storytelling works two ways. David Watt, a pastor with an evangelist's heart from First Baptist in Dartmouth, reminds us that listening to people's stories who make no claim to be Christian is important. "I expect to reach people at their points of crisis. Like a young couple, living common-law, who were struggling with tragedy. The man had faced a death in his workplace. This was a very traumatic thing for him. I was privileged to be there for him at that moment in his life, to listen and share and allow him to tell his story."

The Willingdon Community Church has a long history of expressing both spiritual and social concern. One of their members said with delight: "It's been really exciting to hear the stories that are coming out of our community meetings. When you hear the story of people telling their neighbors, their friends, the people they work with, the stories of how their lives changed because someone cared – it's exciting."

RESPECTING THE FAITH JOURNEY

We have already noted that one of the marks of Future Faith churches is their readiness to accept people. We need to be careful not to confuse accepting people with either approving their choices or agreeing with all their opinions. Acceptance simply allows people to express themselves, physically or verbally, without being evaluated or judged. Attitudes of acceptance are like welcome mats at the doorway. To withhold acceptance from others sends signals that chase people away from any future relationship or potential influence.

Respecting people is quite different from accepting people. Respect requires a value judgment. To signal respect, we must be convinced that people merit the regard and admiration that honest respect requires. We respect people in professions who have put in preparation in order to serve with excellence. We respect car mechanics and computer technicians who can diagnose problems and make the necessary repairs. We extend appreciation and regard to ministers of the gospel who craft sermons that challenge us to new levels of service and obedience if they give evidence of practicing what they preach. Respect is earned.

In human relationships, however, acceptance and respect are reciprocal. Whether the discussion is with people from other world faiths, individuals who claim to be agnostics, or people who are profoundly indifferent to spiritual matters, the laws of life are predictable: accept others and you will be accepted; respect others and you will be respected: judge others and you will be judged by them.

Future Faith churches deliberately nurture non-judgmental attitudes. From the perspective of a man from St. Johns Anglican, "Because the pastor's message is non-judgmental, we're empowered to take the message without being judgmental when we go out into the world."

Although people in Future Faith churches are no more inclined to offer undeserved respect than anyone else in society, they are ready to extend respect to those who demonstrate spiritual interest. And the regard is not just reserved for people showing evidence of movement toward God; many are predisposed to believe that God is already at work in people's lives whether they are aware of it or not. A man from St. Johns Anglican in Edmonton gave an example: "This church has helped me see God in others. I see God in people in the community and in other places, not just in the church." Similar sentiments came from a United Church parishioner: "From when I was little I've always been a spiritual person. But I was never encouraged to live that way. To me the most en-

joyable thing is opening a discussion with somebody new. And lo and behold, I discover they
have spiritual feelings too."

It is unspoken but assumed that Future Faith
churches expect people to be moving toward
God, and they respect that journey. The movement toward God is not viewed as a march or a
parade. Rather, it is assumed that people are at

**Regular
attenders
are confident
about
bringing
people with
them.**

some point on their spiritual journey, and whatever that point
may be, they are accepted, respected and welcomed. A woman
from First Baptist in Dartmouth articulated the point: "We
are allowed to be on our own individual journey and we are
able to do it in whatever way God is leading us to do it."

EXPECTING PEOPLE TO COME TO FAITH

The spiritual journey that Future Faith churches envision
has a destination. Openness toward people does not equate
to a journey into a void. It is expected that people will grow
in faith. Along the way, special efforts are taken to protect
people from taking roads that will lead into spiritual waste-
lands. In particular, Future Faith churches create environments where regular attenders are confident about bringing people with them, and when new people enter, they feel
comfortable.

A man in the focus group at The Meeting Place spoke enthusiastically: "I have confidence that I could take someone
with no church background, or someone that had a negative
church background, and bring them into a service. I can do
so without being worried that I would be ashamed or feeling
I have to cringe at something that was said or done."

Carlin Weinhauer explained that at Willingdon Community they are very intentional about how they relate to

newcomers: "The services are such that you can bring a friend here on Sunday and you know you're not going to be embarrassed. We make no more fuss over people other than asking them to fill out a welcome card – if they're comfortable in doing that." Carlin also acknowledges that "many people have come to Christ who first of all were invited to a Christmas or Easter presentation. So it's really relational evangelism. And people love seeing people saved – especially their friends."

Future Faith churches are blending and augmenting the "come to" mindset of mainline churches and the "go to" strategy of evangelical churches. The experience of a woman from Streetsville Anglican is indicative of other Future Faith churches: "I get the message loud and clear here that our responsibility is to bring more people and introduce them to Christ. And when you sit back and you reflect on your life and how much better it's gotten since you've had this relationship, you do naturally bring people in."

TWO ROADS TO FAITH

On the issue of Christian witness and evangelism, however, matters are not as clear-cut. The lack of clarity does not mean there are churches among the 14 surveyed who lack a concern for inviting people to experience Christ and know God. Rather, there are different understandings and practices about how people establish a relationship with Christ – by words, and by deeds.

Wesley Campbell from the Vineyard is happy to have evangelism take either the deeds route or the words route. Campbell says, "The fact that people are being helped makes me glad; the fact that people are being saved makes me glad."

Talking about her understanding of witnessing, a woman from Grandview Calvary took a different slant. She wouldn't separate the deeds of social care from words of soul care. In her words, "If you don't love me, don't tell me about Jesus." Similar comments from Barry Parker, the rector of St. Johns Anglican, also signal a rising level of complexity: "In Canada, where the social gospel has taken preeminence, often we view evangelism as just going and doing whatever we are doing in the community. I would disagree with that. I think we still need to be concerned about salvation."

The complexity of evangelism transfers into caution – even dissent – with the perspective of Corbin Eddy from Saint Basil's Catholic church: "I'm quite uncomfortable with certain evangelical tendencies. I'm very uncomfortable with somebody putting their hand on somebody's head and then discerning the spirit. I'm just not sure what's happening there or that you are converted to Jesus in that way. I don't know how valid it is, how true it is."

With a typical Canadian regard for both sides of the question, a Christian Reformed participant asked: "What's the appropriate way to witness – in terms of not wanting to turn people off but not wanting to chicken out either?"

Diversity on the subject of evangelism should not surprise us. Within Protestantism, mainline and evangelical churches have long-standing differences. As a universal and demographically expansive church, Catholics are born into the faith and through the influence of home, church and school are nurtured in their life in Christ.

If what is happening in Future Faith churches is an indicator, when it comes to how people are coming to faith and beginning to follow Jesus, we are entering a new stage of evangelistic history. Two comments from lay people, one from a

Christian Reformed member and the other from a Baptist Church participant, reveal both a new direction and a sustained commitment to the gospel.

- *I grew up in a very evangelical church and there were a lot of altar calls for the decision to accept Christ. I have not seen that approach here and I wondered to myself – how do people come to faith? Do people come in already believing or just exactly how does that happen? It's a much more private and subtle way of coming to belief than I was used to.*
- *The Gospel must never be compromised, but the methodology of delivery of the Gospel is constantly evolving here. We're not the world in the church and we don't ever want to be, but we need to be out in the world and be real there. So if it means that we have to go sit in the lesbian bar and talk to people to help us understand the issue of homosexuality, then let's do it.*

Of the 14 Future Faith churches, only a minority see evangelism in the "hour-of-decision Damascus-Road" mode. A strong majority see God relating to people in the journey motif. Rather than emphasizing the need to encounter Christ in a moment, they see the journey of faith as a continuing process. In some of the churches, both views would exist side by side.

THE DAMASCUS ROAD APPROACH

The Damascus Road view of coming to faith (Acts 9:1-9) is certainly a part of some Future Faith churches. Just as Saul, the persecutor, was converted on the road from Jerusalem to Damascus when Jesus dramatically confronted him, some Future Faith people would contend, "That is how people become Christians. There is a moment. There is a time and place when Christ comes and forgives." A Baptist woman was very definite about this: "Conversion is a point where a person realizes their need of a Savior; you're a sinful person and Christ has died for your sins; you accept that, and you claim him as your Lord, and you follow him." Carlin Weinhauer from Willingdon Community affirmed his predecessor for setting the "direction for evangelism. People do need the Lord, and you can win people to Christ. The church has always been creative in trying to develop evangelism ... We emphasize friendship evangelism and event evangelism." The Kelowna Vineyard church has experienced remarkable growth. Pastor Wesley Campbell explained that "in our early days when we started the church, we had two pastors. Within a couple of years, we were over 400 people. We've probably led 1000 to 2000 people to Christ in the last decade. That's a lot of conversions in 12 years."

THE EMMAUS ROAD APPROACH

Evangelism according to the "journey on the Emmaus Road mode" is less definitive. Like the people who walked with Jesus from Jerusalem to Emmaus, they are with Jesus but for a time they do not recognize his full significance. But eventually "their eyes are opened." They recognize Jesus and want him to stay with them. Reflecting on the journey they know "their hearts were burning within" and that something profound is happening to them (Luke 24:13-35 NRSV).

Two Baptist pastors, one younger and one older, speak representatively on the Emmaus mode for other Future Faith clergy. Doug Ward explains: "Evangelism is not secondary here. We've done a lot of baptisms. A lot of people come to Christ here in dramatic ways. But they're ways that don't come through programs or any kind of system. I think I've made an altar call maybe once in the last 2 years." David Watt speaks similarly: "I see myself as an evangelist but helping people make a decision is not that evident for me. It's more working with people and listening to people and praying with people and then watching God work a miracle in their lives. I mean just to be there, to see what God's doing – that's the thrill."

Lay people speak also in Emmaus Road terms. The nuances are distinct from Damascus road language. Their expressions merit careful observation:

- *Jesus Christ? What do we do with him? This church does provide the opportunity to wrestle with Christ wherever you are on the road of faith – whether you've been on the way or whether you're just coming to find out who Jesus is.*
- *I think there's a real trust that God is working here. I really like that a lot.*
- *We're learning to follow. None of us are there. There's really no final stage. We're not expected to be perfect, we're all learning, trying, stumbling, helping each other up. We're learning to follow.*

Future Faith churches are committed to follow Jesus and his ways. They embrace the gospel in its fullness. They are "love God and love your neighbor" people. This participant in a focus group might have been speaking on behalf of all 14 churches: "The whole Gospel is not just helping people who need a meal or a place to sleep. We are also encouraging people to seek Christ, to come to know Christ as their personal savior."

And people who come to know Christ personally see "the Christian life as people living their faith, people living what we learn," as one focus group participant said. "It's not standing on the corner handing out tracts, thumping people on the head saying 'Turn or burn!' People are looking at people and the ministries in this church and saying 'I see God, and I see Jesus Christ in your actions, you are living it.' I mean it's really happening here."

Methodist preacher and author William Willimon would agree with that sentiment:

The gospel is not a set of interesting ideas about which we are supposed to make up our minds. The gospel is intrusive news that evokes a new set of practices, a complex of habits, a way of living in the world, discipleship. The obedience we owe to Christ makes Christianity far more than an ethical code – it is a way of life. It is a way of living as if the Kingdom of God has already come about.[9]

Let us give the final word to David Watt. He hopes that others can live with the same health and wholeness he has experienced. "I like to begin with individuals, so that they can be at peace with themselves and sense they are becoming whole people. I want people to experience wholeness. Unless you are spiritually healthy, unless you have a sense of wholeness, you're not going to be able to function out there with any kind of power ..."

Future Faith churches are a part of God's grand scheme to bring abundant life into the 21st century. They are faithful people of God in the modern world. The ministry model that frames their activity is both biblically grounded and culturally sensitive. It is worthy of being re-produced, adapted to various denominational styles and enhanced.

- Affection for the **heart** through **worship**
- Insight for the **mind** through **learning**
- Behavior for the **hands** through **service**
- Meaning for the **voice** through **witness**

6

NON-NEGOTIABLES FOR
FUTURE FAITH CHURCHES

The church has always been a divine-human creation. Whether the label is Mainline Protestant or Catholic, Orthodox or Evangelical Protestant, Charismatic or independent, human minds and hands have always fashioned what they believed God would have them establish.

As a result, the collective Christian church is a vast assortment of the visions, convictions, wills, and ways of people driven spiritually to do the work of God. We can be certain that on this side of heaven there never will be a church structure and spiritual agenda totally in tune with divine preferences.

In Canada, churches which tend to focus on evangelism and a soul care agenda often are attracted to the teachings of the church growth movement. This movement has provided understanding and techniques that are helpful for churches to reach the secular world. However, the downside is that there has sometimes been little concern for social transformation and Jesus' agenda for the church to care for the needs of the poor.

Other congregations which tend to focus on social connectedness and a social care agenda are often driven by advocacy and change agency movements. Their passion for involvement in justice and equality issues is commendable. But the emphasis may neglect the soul care side of the gospel and too often begs the question of "What is the church meant to be?"

Lacking a clear theology of the church, we can become merely technique-and-program-driven in our congregational development. The temptation often is to look for churches that are accomplishing impressive ministry elsewhere and then attempt to adopt them as prototypes to be reproduced locally.

Future Faith churches build a theological framework for their identity which informs their cultural awareness and enhances their ability to function effectively. They know who they are, where they are located, and when they are in their moment in time. Seeking to reproduce patterns from another church without careful examination of these three essentials leads to church cloning.

DANGERS OF CHURCH CLONING

In the present environment, attempts to manufacture what God is doing in churches in other cities and often in another country are a prevalent pattern. In Canadian evangelical circles, many visions and plans are drowning in efforts to emulate Bill Hybel's Willow Creek congregation. Many other Canadian congregations are attempting to ride the wave of Rick Warren's "California Saddleback purpose-driven church." Like riding a bucking bronco in the Calgary Stampede, they are getting bruised in the dust and dirt of the Canadian turf. No one has an actual count but thousands of clergy and lay observers from all Christian church traditions have visited the Toronto Airport Christian Fellowship (formerly Vineyard) with the hope that the Toronto way could become their way.

Seeking to reproduce patterns from another church leads to church cloning.

In mainline circles, the latest books from the Alban Institute and from Lyle Shaller, with their analyses and recommendations, provide injections of hope. Tutored and stimulated by outside resource people like Bill Easum and Lyman Coleman, many priests and pastors have staked their vocational futures for potential renewal on the promises of the small group movement.

Undoubtedly, there are many valid ministry principles and strategies to pursue in these extraordinary churches. But translating an idea into the flesh and blood of another church is still challenging. Duplicating a church prototype from one community to another faces formidable obstacles. The demographics in communities are too different; every culture is too distinctive to be homogenized. The genuine activity of God's spirit is too strong, too unpredictable, and too independent to be cloned.

Since most of the successful prototypes seem to be in the United States, we often fail to successfully adapt them to the unique contexts of local churches in Canadian neighborhoods. In one example, a talented and personable pastor of a large, growing congregation in Southern California was describing the ingredients for successful churches. His audience sat in a seminar room in Regina, Saskatchewan. Throughout the day-long seminar, the irony of the context was apparent to everyone but him. The pastor promoted his experience of working in an area of over 5 million people, suggesting that the methods would stay the same in Regina with a population of 160,000.

It was a strange experience. Even his measurements of success failed to address the issue of context seriously. Even more frustrating was that while he talked about models and strategies, he never once articulated what the church was called to be.

FLAWED APPROACHES

Because church leaders are often inclined to assume US ministry prototypes will work well for us in Canada, there is a tendency to adopt uncritically these approaches rather than to adapt them to our context. This desire to reproduce what happens elsewhere has often had disastrous results on the church in Canada.

The Canadian congregational scene is made up of many different dynamics. Take a quick survey of the congregations in your district or community. How many of the following five generalizations show up?

- The **Disneyland church** is a popular approach with many congregations. The worship and ministry feels like a blend of *Entertainment Tonight* and attending a sports event. Whether worship features the latest wave of experiential spirituality or the hottest worship team in the city, these churches promise an exciting adventure of faith. Using words like "seeker-sensitive" and "contemporary," they play into the consumer orientation of society and treat church life much like a radio station which changes formats and play lists to be more audience friendly.

  The drive is to be relevant. But the problem for the entertaining, consumer-oriented church is that "tastes" change. In fact, they change so frequently that many congregations find themselves constantly taking on new images and shrugging off old ones. Churches lose their sense of continuity; congregations grow unstable; individuals are confused about who they are to be.

- Then there are **Restaurant churches** which shape their life with the accommodating slogan, "Place your order here." These full menu churches have programs for every age and appetite. If you have a need, they have a program.

    To be effective, a restaurant church requires a critical mass of people. Size and resources are all-important. Smaller congregations offer their own limited menu of activities to compete with larger congregations in much the same way that "mom and pop" neighborhood corner stores compete with the supermarket down the street. The frustration of competing with the big church whose resources are greater and programs more flashy is disheartening. The small church cannot win when success is measured on these terms!

    Too often the menu of restaurant churches includes smaller churches as the daily special. Once a church passes 400 congregants it becomes what Carl George calls a receptor church. He explains that between 75% and 90% of new members to a congregation of 400 plus are transfers from smaller congregations. George counsels would-be restauranteurs that there "exists a widespread notion that North America's medium and large size churches are evangelistic centers ... These churches are by and large centers for reprocessing believers ... that throng to them from smaller churches."[1]

- **Teaching center churches** are another form you may notice. In contrast to the Disneyland or restaurant churches, these congregations set themselves as beacons of clarity in the midst of the ambiguity. They are antidotes to the relativity of today's society. Marked with gifted and authoritative teaching, they sound a certain and final word of authority to people awash in changing times.

In their isolated classrooms, these churches teach stability. But they do not always mirror a true reflection of the world around them. They provide a sure base, but only to those who are prepared to adopt the life they espouse.

Some might consider only looking for teaching center congregations among the evangelical churches which are often labeled conservative fundamentalist. But fundamentalism relates to prejudices whether they are conservative or liberal. Liberal churches can carry their own brand of liberal fundamentalism. Whether conservative or liberal, fundamentalists are the same – they are both stuck. One has the window stuck open, the other has the window closed – that's the only difference.

Teaching center churches subtly tell you that faith is about information and a particular experience. People take notes to think better. In this "information in – information out" orientation to the faith, congregational members subtly assume that the more you know, the more Christian you will be in your lifestyle and responsibilities. Although knowledge is crucial, integration of that knowledge is essential for the transformation of people to become integrated disciples of Christ.

- A fourth church type, easy to spot in most communities, is **Hothouse churches**. They emphasize life together, asking people to bring themselves and their families into the fellowship. Hothouse churches are relationally intense places where the family concept of church creates a navel gazing conformity.

  The call to commitment becomes exclusive. You are either in or you are out. If you are not ready to commit to the level that hothouse churches require, they find it difficult to include you. If you don't fit the family characteristic, then you will know you don't belong.

Liberal churches can carry their own brand of liberal fundamentalism.

Hothouse churches are intense in their call to life together. They take pride in separating themselves from the world. Their members are expected to work for a living but one of the primary purposes of making money is to supply the needed resources to support the ministry of their church.

- Finally, **Community League churches** are also popular, particularly in busy urban centers. Service is their specialty. They place few demands and bring few expectations to their life together. As they throw their doors open to anybody in their rush to be of service, they become landlords to many organizations and service clubs.

  Community League churches lack self-definition and values. Community League churches exist for others and are defined in the milky motto, "What do you want us to do for you?" Often they lack a passion for the inner life of spirituality. They miss the Spirit which should fuel their acts of service.

MORE THAN ONE WAY TO BE THE CHURCH

Whichever church types show up in your community, it will be obvious that different models have different strengths and weaknesses. Some are growing communities with genuine hope and vibrancy. Some take pride in emphasizing the importance of soul care while others take just as much pride in extolling social care. But in most instances, a closer examination reveals they are struggling because of their unexamined and flawed strategies.

We know that geographic areas are different. Vancouver is not Halifax and Edmonton is not Toronto, and Rock Creek is "none of the above." In Canadian society, we find people from a variety of cultures, religious and ethnic groups. The reality of cultural pluralism makes our neighborhoods socially and morally complex places.

To be effective, Canadian churches need to deal with an array of differences. It is no wonder that churches often find it difficult to translate these complexities into clear strategies for church ministry and mission. Like the person at the lottery ticket counter waiting for the "big win," church leadership often spend a lot of energy looking for the magic cure. Slipping easily into what urban missiologist Ray Bakke calls "a McDonald's Franchise" church mindset,[2] they ignore the reality of context, tradition and culture hoping to find the one-size-fits-all solution.

Searching for answers to the dilemma of Canadian church life, ministers and lay leaders do the circuit. They attend seminars, workshops, pray for revival, and read the latest books. Seminars, whether by evangelical or mainline resource people, tell them that the church must be more "audience sensitive." To solve the problem of congregational life and outreach in the 1990s, they are told to understand who is out there and what they need. Find a need and fill it. The philosophy, we fear, reflects our consumer economy more than it does the gospel of Jesus Christ.

The suggestions do have some merit. A marketing mentality creates a deeper sensitivity to non-church people, spawning congregations that understand who they are trying to reach with the gospel. The emphasis focuses congregations outside of themselves and engenders attitudes that are mission minded. At its worst, though, the marketing mentality traps congregations in the fantasy that mere technique and programs will provide the miracle cure. The church simply mirrors culture in a desperate attempt to be relevant to the audience.

This marketing approach has produced churches who, desiring relevance and social connectedness, lose the prophetic role of the people of God by capitulating to culture. A marketing orientation also nurtures churches that root themselves in the cultural excesses of radical individualism and materialism in an attempt to win souls trapped in these very excesses. Neither expression of the church requires the work of the Spirit in transforming people into the image of Christ. Instead, it tickles the cultural tendencies of modern humanity.

Whatever their dominant denominational label or theological framework, the Future Faith churches included in this study illustrate the reality that one size does not fit all. Small or large, community oriented or regionally focused, non-traditional or traditional in style, what they share in common causes them to stand apart from most churches in Canada today.

DEFINABLE DIFFERENCES

Future Faith churches aren't perfect but they are different. Each of them has found their own unique way to relate their faith tradition to the people around them. They have a sense of self-confidence about who they are, and an ability to stand firm in that identity – even if doing so puts them out of step with their denomination and neighboring churches.

Future Faith churches find common ground in their ability to balance the soul care priorities of building personal faith with community ministry commitments that express redemptive social care. By learning about their neighborhoods, they speak to the contexts in which they are located. They shape that knowledge into ministry and mission without losing sight of the distinct nature of the gospel they serve.

Future Faith churches create an atmosphere of acceptance for all people but realize that life with Christ and his church cannot be based on human opinions alone. They long for quantitative growth which is essential to the on-going life of any congregation. But they also understand growth in qualitative terms. They are concerned that the lives of their congregants reflect more and more the character and depth of the gospel's demands on people's lives.

Knowing WHO You Are

The constant factor in effective churches is not size, worship style, church tradition, or even theological flavor, but a deep belief about what the church is biblically mandated to be. Future Faith churches know who they are. They function with a clear identity, a clear self-image. As a result, they are purpose motivated. Loren Mead observes that currently "we are in a time when we are not looking for cosmetic changes, [but looking at] our identity as people of God, with how we live together, with what our environment really is."[3]

Terry Ingram asks, "How do we institutionally help people be what they are supposed to be out there?" He explains that the answer is based on understanding who we are and why we are here. "In other words," Ingram states, "we have a minimal amount of structures which are here to keep this institution functioning, not just for the sake of keeping it functioning but so that people can gather to worship and mature as God's people wherever they are found. That is different than hatching a program to make it Christian. It is an orientation and mindset about 'who we are' as the church."

NON-NEGOTIABLES FOR FUTURE FAITH CHURCHES • 177

The constant factor in effective churches is not size, worship style, church tradition, or even theological flavor.

Understanding who we are creates an atmosphere which allows congregations to develop ministry and mission with confidence. James Fowler notes that "when the spine of identity is well established, it is possible to risk relating in depth to those who are different from ourselves."[4] Future Faith congregational life authenticates the words they speak and as a result are able to reach out to people different from themselves.

Future Faith churches know they are a people gathered around a particular event. An intervention has come from God in the person of Jesus Christ; Christians are called to witness to that event. Future Faith congregations are fueled by their desire to witness to the Incarnation (Colossians 3:12-17). They picture a people of God mobilized in the so-called secular world, living authentic lives in the places they work, play and connect. The writer of the first letter of Peter likens this call to the mobilizing of a holy priesthood (1 Peter 2:4-5). A particular and peculiar people are called into being as a new social order – radically and revolutionarily different. This congregational identity has a direct impact on what the church looks like and how it shapes its mission.

Rodney Clapp prophetically calls for churches to live rooted in the certainty of knowing who they are when he writes that churches should be distinctive and live by their understanding of being a community, constituted and sustained by Christ. He concludes, "According to that very self-definition, the church does not exist for itself, but for its mission and witness to the world on behalf of the kingdom."[5]

Stanley Hauerwas and William Willimon speak to the same issue in their book *Resident Aliens*. Speaking out of their roots as American Methodists, they say that through the gift of faith and vision grounded in Jesus Christ the church knows that its most credible form of witness is creating a living, breathing, visible community of faith. The authors explain that churches should seek to be "a place, clearly visible to the world, in which people are faithful to their promises, love their enemies, tell the truth, honor the poor, suffer for righteousness and thereby testify to the amazing community-creating power of God."[6]

Matthew, Mark, and Luke all state that to be the faithful people of God, we need to place the "reign of God" at the center of our thought and action. Using a "kingdom" motif, these three gospel writers use similar words and themes to describe what Jesus has come to do – usher in the reign of God with a new way of living and relating. Jesus' mission has been taken up by the church but, too often in the last decades, the "reign of God" theology has been preempted with a theology that turns the church into an end unto itself. Rather than a vehicle of mission which makes possible God's redemptive plan, the survival and growth of the church have become the goal.

The church is more than a "holy huddle." Stan Grenz notes this difference when he says that the church is not an end in itself. Rather, he writes, today's church "exists to serve a larger intention. The Spirit forms us into a people through whom [the Spirit] can bring about the completion of God's work in the world. This suggests that we must be a future oriented people. Our task is directed toward a grand goal which will come into its fullness only at the end of the age ... To understand this, we must introduce the biblical drama of God at work establishing the kingdom or reign. Indeed, the church initially emerged in the context of Jesus' announcement, 'The kingdom of God is near.' (Mark 1:15)."[7]

NOT A ONE-SIDED CHRISTIANITY

In the polarization of Canadian church life, we continue to debate God's primary concern for the church. Claiming to speak for God, one church orientation declares our primary mandate is soul care through the proclamation and evangelism. The other side declares a priority for social connectedness through seeking justice and responding to needs in the community. Tragically, the theological concept of reestablishing God's reign over all of creation has been relegated to the biases of one-sided theologies. The result has been the creation of one-sided faith people.

Ronald Sider assumes that the Bible is God's word and he believes Jesus spoke truth. On this basis he argues in his latest book, *One-Sided Christianity*, that every church should be "equipping its people for the work of evangelism, praying constantly for the salvation of sinners and regularly – month by month – experiencing the joy of welcoming new members into the circle of Jesus' redeemed community." Then he adds that every church should also be "immersed in service to the hurting and broken in their own world. That kind of church would end the scandal of one-sided Christianity."[8]

Future Faith churches believe they must live out the concerns of the reign of God that are mandated by a double-edged faith. This double-edged faith acknowledges the spiritual implications of personal sin as well as the economic systemic and social sins that sustain injustice and inequity in society. They understand the power of a reconnected Gospel. They celebrate the occasions when people repent and exchange their spiritual alienation for forgiveness and new life in Christ. They believe their relationship with God will sustain them and that there is eternal life after death. They also believe with Roger Mitchell his message from *The King-*

dom Factor. "The work of the kingdom is not so much to get people out of earth into heaven, but to get as much heaven onto this earth and into people."[9]

The current political climate gives a high priority to economic concerns. Many in the church have joined with voices clamoring for economic responsibility and even for tax relief, but have failed to address how the church will deal with a society in which government is no longer responsible for justice and poverty priorities concerns. Jim Wallis speaks powerfully to our need to respond as Christians. He says:

In the cries and prayers of the poor, we will hear the spiritual call of our time. Though most today would consider the idea foolish, the point of this gospel passage (Matthew 25) is that our future is with the poor; our destinies are tied together, one way or another. Despite the many noises of this society that distract our attention, assault our minds, and harden our hearts, we have a very real stake in one another's lives. And the circumstances of the most vulnerable among us are always the best test of our human solidarity with one another.[10]

A DISTINCT IDENTITY

Future Faith churches focus on forming a distinct identity. They emphasize theological concepts that acknowledge the work of the Holy Spirit in their personal lives. Church members are equipped and encouraged to live as the people of God in their cultural contexts. During our research for this book, one focus participant said, "the key ingredient in the church is all of us. The church is not just a meeting place for programs to go out and serve the hungry and minister to needs. It is people who have a sense of call. An encouragement to have our eyes opened in such a way as to create a compassionate heart which gets involved in the community."

Knowing who they are, Future Faith churches develop an identity focused on the reign of God. They become purpose motivated. Their identity enables them to strike a balance of responsibility between a soul-based spirituality and a social-based spirituality. Their personal faith in Jesus Christ generates a concern for the particular needs of people around them. They worship intimately and live differently! Marva Dawn writes of this radical identity when she says, "Our faith story is that of God's self-giving presence and intervention which calls us and forms us to be a community in response ... Christ came for this people, lived among people, chose people to carry on his mission, died for people. His chosen people were gathered when the Holy Spirit came to empower them for ministry to every other people."[11]

Knowing WHERE You Are

As well as knowing who they are, Future Faith churches know where they are. Their ministries are context specific. Although they embody and express forms of faith compatible with their denominational affiliations, they also respond to specific conditions in their communities. They are sensitive about circumstances in their neighborhoods. Demographic characteristics, socio-economic factors, and the presence of ethnic diversity, all influence what these churches do and how they do it. Programs, worship styles, and the atmosphere of church life are all affected by where they are.

One woman in a focus group described the preaching at her church. Speaking of her minister, she said, "He is just so real with issues. He talks about the issues like he really knows our city. He knows the demographic issues that concern people and gears his sermons around them."

Describing her excitement with the church she attended, another focus group participant told us, "I tell friends who ask me about the church that this is a church for today's people. They address real issues that we face every day. I am always telling them that the sermon often starts with a quote from the front page of today's newspaper. It is not just about history, it is really applicational stuff and stimulating."

Future Faith congregations see people outside the church as a field of influence. They know they are called both to witness and to serve as ambassadors of the living Christ (2 Corinthians 5:11-21). Their neighborhoods provide the faces and relationships in which their faith is expressed. The atmosphere of the church reflects the knowledge that they are to embody the servant attitudes of Christ (Philippians 2:1-11). As a result, these churches intentionally reach out to their communities. As Daniel Olson puts it, they have an "outward orientation."[12]

This outward orientation has two primary dimensions. There is a geographical or community connectedness. And there is an interpersonal or relational connectedness.

GEOGRAPHICAL CONNECTEDNESS

Unfortunately many Canadian churches function with indifference to the context around them and end up as subcommunities in their neighborhoods. Their worship and ministry life appear unrelated to the rhythms of their geographical neighbors. Insulated from and cut off from the issues in their neighborhoods, these churches launch occasional forays into the community in attempts to attract nonattenders.

Future Faith churches do not view themselves as disconnected from the everyday life in the neighborhoods where they are located. They take seriously such biblical mandates as Jeremiah 29:4-9 where the prophet calls the people of God to "seek the peace and well-being of the city." Therefore, the neighborhoods where they are present become a specific focus for their mission endeavors.

Geographic connectedness is demonstrated by Tim Dickau at Grandview Community Church. He talks enthusiastically about the commitment within their church to run literacy programs and offer English as a second language (ESL) resources to their east side inner-city neighborhood in Vancouver. He loves visiting people where they work and asks questions like, "What would it mean to love the people here and reflect Christ in this neighborhood?" He explains that this "is not about what we do at the church building or what we do when we are gathered together. There is a growing sense that we are people called into this community."

Another example of geographical connectedness is found in a small parish based church within Edmonton's Highlands community. Taking their neighborhood commitment seriously, they responded to needs in an elementary school across the street from their building. The church has partnered with the school in food nutrition, recess supervision and volunteer management. The experiment has been so successful that the Edmonton School Board has sought to use this example as one that can be reproduced throughout the city. The result has been a healthier school environment. And the intentional involvement by the church in the community has brought new levels of life to the congregation.

Future Faith churches have a "theology of place." Creative partnerships emerge and ministries that meet real needs in the life of the neighborhood result. Church and community are linked in surprising ways and congregations discover a renewed place in community life.

RELATIONAL CONNECTEDNESS

Not all congregational members live in the communities where they worship. That is a reality of church life. Churches that treat only the places where their buildings are located as their mission field miss a crucial dimension – people's lives are not limited to geographical locations. Throughout the week congregational members interact with numerous people who represent a field of mission contact for the church when it is dispersed. Whether they are neighbors, business colleagues, friends in leisure, or family members, these people offer relationships of significance where faith can be lived out and made real.

The opportunities are not only an urban church phenomenon. Rural and small town churches have the same dynamic. A friend who is a pastor in a rural church serves as an agricultural consultant to farmers in the area around his church. His undergraduate degree in agriculture provides a resource for networking the community spread over a large area around the church he leads.

Participants in our research focus groups echoed this understanding. They indicate that they develop an outward orientation through relationship building. A participant described the various outreaches her church performs in their community. She highlighted the work of a food cupboard, housing for the homeless, and a hospice. She says these are signs that her church is "actually living what we are told to do. We are not saying 'you have to be a Christian before we can help you, or you have to live our way before we are going to help you with our church.' Neither are we saying 'you have to come to our church before we are going to help you.' All that help comes from what God is commanding us to do in the Bible first, and then you see people coming through the doors."

People's lives are not limited to geographical locations.

Jeff Woods thinks this is a good formula for church life because it builds solid relationships. He explains that people primarily want to feel connected and that they want to know the church cares. About newcomers to a church, Woods says, "People want to be introduced and be invited to hear more about God from people who are already friends. People in the church need to appear to others as being caring and compassionate. The entire church should also give that signal."[13] The only way that happens is if people inside the church live in touch with the people outside the church who make up the tapestry of their lives.

Knowing where your church is creates a place to which people connect and belong. Church members know people who have nothing to do with institutional and religious life. Their hurts and needs are not just theory, because these members share in the lives of their neighbors every day. One focus group member described the time that he learned a friend had died of AIDS and then the next day learned about another friend who has AIDS. This participant was grateful he was part of a church that could hear his pain and support him with these painful realities. "Being part of this kind of church," he says, "allows me to live in the world that I am in. To live in the real world with my feet rooted in tradition and my heart rooted in faith."

Knowing WHEN You Are

Future Faith churches also know when they are. They are culturally alert. They are in touch with the times. They understand where the church is positioned within the dominant culture. Rather than being intimidated by the world around them, Future Faith people are ready to be what they claim to be. They are less likely to react and more likely to live with informed anticipation.

Here's a story – possibly fictional – that illustrates the need to be culturally alert. A couple were hiking in high mountain meadows in the early summer. They came upon a vast area of mushrooms. Knowing that some mushrooms can be poisonous, they studied them closely and, declaring them fit for eating, filled their backpacks with the edible delights.

Coming down the mountain, they planned a great "Mushroom Feast" for their friends. They sent out invitations, set out the menus, and prepared for the day. The joyful group feasted on mushroom quiche, stuffed mushrooms, and various other mushroom delights. Finally they settled in the living room for the digestive banter of conversation.

All of a sudden, a crash came from the kitchen. They rushed to see what had interrupted their revelry. To their horror, they saw the family cat lying on the floor, gasping for breath, below the counter where they had left the mushroom dishes. She had apparently been nibbling on leftovers and had fallen in convulsions on the floor. One guest articulated what they were all thinking: "The mushrooms must be bad!"

They packed into cars and raced to the hospital where their stomachs were pumped and they were held in observation for a few hours. Finally, they were all released and allowed to go home. Because many of them had left their coats at the couple's house, they returned to pick them up. After humorously thanking their hosts for a great evening, they began to leave. Then one of them remembered the cat. She was nowhere to be seen. But they heard a meow from behind the stove. They took a look. Expecting to see a cat that was almost dead, they peered into the space. There they saw the cat – with six little kittens crowded around her.[14]

The moral of the story is, check the signals.

People who understand the times read everything that is happening around them with inquiring eyes. They understand that society is changing. To be effective, they seek to interpret accurately the signals being sent by the culture around them (2 Timothy 4:1-6). Until recently, although we espoused a mosaic appreciation, people in Canada were primarily homogenous. Christianity was the dominant religious and cultural voice in society. But times have changed.

FACING CONTINUOUS CHANGE

Alan Roxburgh understands the challenge Canadian churches face as they approach the 21st century. In his thoughtful book, *Reaching a New Generation,* he declares, "North American churches have lost touch with the incredible changes that have been transforming our culture over the past 25 years. Consequently we are ill-prepared to speak the gospel into the world taking shape around us."[15]

Eddie Gibb's book, *In Name Only: Tackling the Problem of Nominal Christianity,* refers to the secularizing influences in the culture. In Canada, although many people still feel they need the church for rites of passage or in times of crisis, they are not regular participants. Gibbs advises that churches who want to regain influence in a less responsive urban society must deal with the "realization that a church designed to meet the ministry needs of the 1950s and 1960s is unlikely to make it through the 1990s unless it is prepared to undergo some fundamental changes."[16]

Someone noted that living in the last decade of the 20th century is like living in a never-ending home renovation. Change is the order of the day. Observers such as Roxburgh and Gibbs tell us is that the gap between society and church has grown wider. There is a fatal flaw in thinking that the only thing churches have to do is tinker with style and program, rather than change the way we relate to the people around us. Jeff Woods acknowledges, "Society has changed. The church now finds itself in the precarious position of responding to the needs of a changed society. Unless the church is committed to a constant struggle to appeal to the world around it, it will fail in its efforts to be the church in the world."[17]

We can see one example of Wood's acknowledgment in the spiritual climate of the day. We live in an age when people are more sensitive and open to dialogue about spirituality and transcendence. Even young people today express an openness to God, but at the same time express a growing distrust of the institutional church. Churches that signal they have some understanding of life beyond their own four walls will be in the best position to provide a place for exploration. One woman in a focus group put it well: "the Gospel is never compromised, but the methodology of delivery is constantly evolving."

A minister currently serving a church in Vancouver regularly meets with young adults (18-25 years of age) in group discussion. The only criterion for these meetings is that the participants be disconnected from church life. He believes that if you are going to speak in any meaningful way to the so-called next generation, you must know what motivates them, what values they hold, and what strikes passionately at their hearts. He realizes that with that knowledge they will be able to speak a meaningful word to their lives.

FROM CHRISTENDOM TO CULTURAL PLURALISM

We live in a time when our words are authenticated more by actions than anything else. Perhaps this change in society has had the greatest impact on the church in Canada. In times past, our words could be spoken and people would listen. Our words needed no other authentication than the authority granted by our place in society. There was no need to flesh those words out in action. We only had to speak, because we lived and felt like a majority voice that must be heard.

Mike Regele in *Death of the Church* discusses this in an interesting way. He writes that in the "Christendom paradigm," society uses its local resources to further the expansion of the kingdom of God at home and abroad. But today, Regele notes, "There is no Christian society any longer. In the emerging postmodern era of religious pluralism, mission is next door and across the street."[18]

The tension of the loss of the Christendom paradigm roots us in the need to relate differently to the world around us. Peter Coots, associate minister at Oakridge Presbyterian Church in London, understands the tension. He says, "In a postmodern world, you can no longer assume the Christendom model. It becomes more imperative to figure out what it is that we really stand for. There is no longer a meshing of church and culture. We have to relate to the culture in a different way." He is right. Cultural pluralism requires a new set of rules of listening and relating that resonate more with New Testament times than ever before. Future Faith churches understand the crucial differences illustrated by the following chart.

Rules and rituals for Christendom	Rules and rituals for cultural pluralism
God is supreme. God's ways matter to most people.	God is just one of many alternatives. Individuals decide what matters most.
Church is at the center of society. Church is respected. Culture delivers people to church. Clergy are chaplains to the culture.	Church competes with other options. Church must earn respect. Local churches become prototypes. Quality of clergy leadership is crucial.
Truth exists as an assumption. Absolutes for morality exist. Some behaviors right/others are wrong. Biblical norms rule. Heterosexual family is uncontested. Christian ideals are to be practiced.	Truth is a matter of personal opinion. Moral dogmatism is a vice. Multiple moralities coexist. Personal choice controls. New family forms emerge. Reciprocity governs civil society.
Governments get authority from God. Crown and cross link. State/church collaborations abound. Orthodoxy shapes public policy.	Govt's poll/get authority from people. Crown and the cross separate. State controls, Church marginalized. Social debate rages.
Christian voice dominates culture. One way thinking pervades. Diversity is tolerated.	Multi-voices compete in culture. Many ways to believe flourish. Tolerance is a virtue.

Whether we like it or not, the rules have changed. Pluralism has created an atmosphere in which churches can flourish only if they are willing to give up the cultural arrogance with which they have lived for so long. They now find themselves as one of many competing voices needing to recapture their New Testament roots as a minority movement in culture. Christian voices need to be heard, but their influence will be directly linked to their ability to work and live within the new paradigm of cultural pluralism.

NON-NEGOTIABLES FOR FUTURE FAITH CHURCHES

Churches that understand the implications of who they are, when they are and where they are, can find their way into effectiveness. Knowing who we are secures an identity which presents a clear difference between the church as the people of God and the people of the world they are trying to reach. It defines their reason for existence and produces motivation with

purpose. Being context specific and culturally alert will position churches to live within the diversity of today's society while
helping to bring the reign of God into our broken world.

The unique faces of the Future Faith churches which we have
had the privilege of profiling, illustrates how these three ministry non-negotiables interact with each other. When the ministry dynamics of knowing who, when and where you are
converge, churches are able to pursue both soul care and social care.

Love for God generates compassion for people. The power
of the reconnnected gospel is experienced. Churches become
communities of God's people on spiritual journeys which
integrate life and faith in a continuous whole. Father Corbin
Eddy from Ottawa stated it clearly: "I try to help people understand that feeding the hungry and being fed at the Eucha-
rist table is really the same thing. It is the same underlying
spirit that makes it one."

7

FAITH FIT FOR THE FUTURE

We are in a transitional time in history. Both in society and in the church, we are not what we were and there is uncertainty about where we are going. We do know that "the church has lost its role as the keystone in the arch of culture,"[1] but in the realm of defining beliefs, clarifying values, gifting society with moral direction, and mobilizing community compassion in the nation – no other institution or organized social influence is taking its place. We are living in times marked not only by moral ambiguity but also with spiritual yearning. Past desires for certainty are being replaced with coping mechanisms to deal with the certainty of uncertainty. We are feeling fragile.

A PAIR OF CONTRASTS

A couple of years ago I [Don] was invited to participate in an annual regional conference of The United Church of Canada. My role was to make some opening remarks, serve as a theological reflector, and offer concluding observations.

The delegates at the conference were obviously pleased to be present. I remember being impressed with the sounds of laughter, the engaging conversations, and the overall sense of vitality that was evident. The worship was carefully orchestrated, focused, and uplifting. There was a sense of celebration in the mood of the event. I could not help but notice how careful everyone was to be gender inclusive. During the open forum, there was a call to revisit the issue of ordaining homosexuals. The debate was carefully controlled to give both sides a fair hearing. The agenda also dealt with social concerns including a call for more government commitment in support of children in daycare. I cheered their social care.

In the midst of the business, in the worship and in the responses from the theological reflectors, there were many references to "God as creator." Some of the music lifted up and affirmed "native spirituality." Whether it was intentional or more a reflection of the essence of their faith, I couldn't help but notice that there was an absence of Christology. It was only in the ordination service where the historical liturgy was used that the person of Jesus Christ was overtly acknowledged.

As I walked away from the event, I felt certain that I had spent time with some of God's committed and gifted people. I appreciated what was present in the conference, but I also wondered why some emphases were absent.

A couple of weeks later I was in the southern US leading a workshop at the North American Conference for Itinerant Evangelists. My assigned role was to present a workshop on sharing the gospel in a secular society. Evangelists and their spouses had come from every corner of North America and they were ready to soar. The first night had a rally atmosphere and expectations were high. You could feel the energy in the

hall. I sat up in the bleacher seats feeling a little like an ob-
server. Still, the singing stirred my spirit. The preaching affirmed both the continuing role of the evangelist in the modern world and the enduring power of the gospel. Christ was
lifted up. The destructiveness of sin, the importance of the
cross, the death and resurrection of Jesus were all accentu-
ated. I cheered their soul care.

In the program, the "Gaithers" were the featured music
group. They sang their way through several rousing numbers, but the one I particularly remember was, "What God
needs is a *man* – a righteous *man*, a righteous *man.*" Close to
where I sat, several younger women were obviously enjoying the musical experience. I wanted to go over to them and
apologize for the lack of gender sensitivity. But as I assessed
how much they seemed to be celebrating the occasion I wondered if they would share my views or my concern. By the
time the benediction was pronounced, the audience had forgotten about most of their worries. Their spirits had been
touched by God's spirit.

I thought that if there is any group of ministers that needs
encouragement these days, it must be full time evangelists.
For them, I uttered a "thanks be to God." But still, although it
was for different reasons, I had some of the same feelings in
my spirit as I did at the United Church event. I appreciated
much of what was present but I was also disappointed by
what was absent.

Before I went to sleep that night, my mind linked the United
Church conference experience to the night with the Itinerant
Evangelists. My conclusion is an example of part of the motivation for writing this book. The United Church and the Itinerant Evangelists really need each other. While retaining their
emphasis on God as Creator and their agenda of social con-

cerns, if the United Church would give increased attention to Jesus' invitation to live in a personal relationship, they would be more faithful to the gospel. The Itinerant Evangelists' strength is on the soul side of the faith ledger but their neglect of the social side leaves them with a deficient view of the gospel they so valiantly proclaim. Both the United Church and the Itinerant Evangelists could invest their energies in affirming a more complete version and vision of the gospel.

BOTH SIDES OF THE EQUATION

Our intent in this book has been to affirm both sides of the gospel equation – personal faith in Christ and social concern for people in need. Our strategy has not been to criticize the side of faith that is present in church life, but to lament the side of faith that is absent. We believe that extolling a personal faith in Christ without also emphasizing an expression of social concern lacks biblical integrity. Similarly, we believe that the gospel is compromised and people are betrayed when the faith is weighted toward serving the poor and addressing issues of justice without grounding the people of God in their personal relationship with Jesus Christ.

Coins are minted with two distinct sides. The result is beauty in design and a clear identity. A pair of scissors can only cut when the two sharp edges come together. Birds gracefully soar through the sky because they have two wings.

The gospel has two sides too. One side invites a personal love for God; the other side generates compassion for people. In communities of faith and in the lives of individuals, when both sides are embraced, spiritual transformation and social transformation are the result.

Know WHO We Are

We can find our way in this transitional time in history. We can frame our existence as church communities and individual followers of Jesus with a strong measure of confidence and a sense of direction. We may still feel fragile at times and there will be situations where certainty will elude us but we can live with assurance and clarity. In the midst of moral ambiguity and many voices saying, "Come to me, believe in me," we can know who we are. Not only can we resolve the spiritual yearning in our inner spirits, we can invite others to explore our faith journeys with us.

BE CLEARLY CHRISTIAN

There are challenges to resolve in our modern age. When uncertainty is the norm, living with clarity is not a matter of simply putting our spiritual lives on automatic pilot. In order to be decisive, one must be deliberate.

Scholar and author Stanley Hauerwas warns the church and the people of God to be decisive and deliberate about keeping Christ central. He is particularly concerned that the pluralistic spirit of the age is leading the Christian church toward spiritual syncretism. As an antidote to blending and blurring what once were the distinctives of the Christian faith with other views and beliefs, Hauerwas illustrates his concern by comparing a seminary student with a medical student.[2]

First, think about a seminary student studying for the ministry. There are clear curriculum requirements. However, the seminary student is progressive in her thinking and wants to be in tune with the latest ministry trends. She reasons that relational ministry is essential in this age. She thinks to herself, "How can you minister to people if you do not under-

198 • FUTURE FAITH CHURCHES

stand their inner needs and emotional make up?" Accordingly she concludes, "I would prefer studying about interpersonal relationships rather than taking courses in Christology." She goes to the dean and asks: "Instead of the course requirements on Christology, can I go across campus to the psychology department and take equivalent courses in counseling?"

Now, think of a medical student studying to be a surgeon. The medical student is also in touch with the times. He has read the latest articles on holistic medicine. He is convinced that it is important to understand the connectedness of the psychological and the physical realms of human reality. He knows he will need to relate to his patients as people and affirm their dignity in every way. The medical student knows that the curriculum requires courses on anatomy. But he goes to the dean of the medical school and proposes: "Let me go across campus to the psychology department and substitute courses on human development and counseling in place of the courses on anatomy."

At this point, Hauerwas shouts, "This is nonsense!"

Then he catches his breath and says with wisdom: "What anatomy is to medical surgery, Christology is to Christianity."

Future Faith churches are not embarrassed about being clearly Christian. Without judging others, they are unapologetic about the call to follow Christ and live responsibly as people of faith. They are also convinced that Jesus is unique in a much deeper way than just being different – in the same way that every human being is different and unique.

COPING WITH SECULAR PRESSURES
Kirk Hadaway and David Roozen have written a helpful book on revitalizing mainline congregational life. They note that

for churches "to grow and to continue growing, it is necessary for each mainstream church
to become a vital religious institution, vibrant
with the presence of God. It must develop a
clear religious identity, a compelling religious
purpose, and a coherent sense of direction
that arises from that purpose."[3]

**Churches that
lose their
religious and
spiritual
purpose, limp
along in a
desperate
attempt to
survive.**

Church people in Canada sometimes think
the struggle to nurture vital congregational life
is caused by the climate of society and its secularizing forces. The problem, however, is much deeper. Like
Pogo in the cartoon strip who said "We have met the enemy
and he is us," too often we have participated in creating the
atmosphere for our own demise as the church. In our capitu-
lation to culture and in our desire to be relevant, we have
given people too many reasons not to go to church. We have
given up our distinctive voice.

In contrast, Future Faith churches stick to the business of
providing ways to explore spirituality inside the church. They
know people are searching for transcendence, and they provide fertile ground for that exploration to take place. First
and foremost, they believe the church is the creation of God
and a place to find God.

Churches that lose their religious and spiritual purpose
are powerless. They limp along in a desperate attempt to survive. Future faith people celebrate the spiritual and religious
purpose of the church. Barry Parker from St. John's Anglican
is an example. When asked about his most significant achievement as a minister, he replied, "Giving people permission to
know Jesus Christ."

Church leaders insecure about their religious and spiritual convictions will fail to be transformational in their lead-

ership. They have nothing distinctive to invite people to become. Episcopalian Robert Capon is controversial in style but he is also right to assert that the test for the church is to ask: "Is it sufficiently *unacceptable* to the world? Is it *non-religious* enough to get the church out of its 20-century-long love affair with religious respectability?"[4] Whether it is 1920, 1940, 1960, or the year 2020, the mandate of the Christian church is to be clearly Christian. That includes affirming the uniqueness of Christ. The motivation to do so is not just because Jesus is part of the required Christian curriculum. Rather, without the uniqueness of Jesus Christ, the Christian faith falls into an abyss of quandary and theory without plausibility and credibility. Both soul care and social care are deactivated.

BE HONEST ABOUT RELATIVE CERTAINTY

Deciding what to believe about the uniqueness of Jesus is a symbol of our responsibility for making choices. "In the beginning," when "God created the heavens and the earth," God did not intend to force women and men to do what God knows is true and best (Genesis 1:1). Instead, to make human dignity possible, God granted all humanity the right and responsibility to make choices.

Whether we evaluate political views and options or look at the broad range of Christian church alternatives in Canadian society, we see the consequences of how God fashioned creation. We are faced with inescapable choices. We can see this characteristic of creation illustrated in the Canadian political situation today. Canadians are pulled in many directions by choices about the future of this country. Dominant political forces still see Canada from a historic perspective – a country with a strong central voice responding to Francophone and Anglophone agendas as well as multicultural concerns. Another view, espoused by separatists, affirms the makeup of the nation around two cultural groups – one French speaking and the other English speaking. The claim of "unique status" drives their right to separate. Other voices from the West envision Canada as a federation of provinces. The call is to be equal among equals. The debate depicts the struggle. Modern Canada charts its future without a dominant story to gather us together.

The church story in the nation parallels the political divisions and necessitates choices too. In the beginning, two dominant faith traditions landed as a part of our dual linguistic identities. French and Catholic went together, as did English and Protestant. The double separation of language and religion effectively nurtured the nation into "two solitudes." Until the cultural upheaval in the 1960s, Catholics in Quebec had enormous social presence and political power. During the same period of history in English-speaking Canada, mainline Protestants exerted a strong cultural presence.

Just as new political parties have sought the confidence of the Canadian electorate, on the Protestant side of the faith ledger new religious voices have called for commitment. Particularly since the end of World War II, evangelical churches have emerged with increasing strength, vitality, and diversity. Just as the long-established political parties viewed their upstart opposition with a supercilious air, mainline Protestants looked at evangelical churches with a sense of religious superiority. In the current milieu, where mainline churches are often in decline and evangelical churches are in many instances growing, the opposite is happening – a regrettable evangelical spiritual arrogance is emerging.

Whether we look at modern life through a political lens or a religious lens, we no longer have a "grand story" that informs us about who we are or who we are going to be. Instead, we are faced with an increasing plethora of stories with different plot lines. In religious terms, we have a competition for truth. We are faced with determining which plot line in the different church stories is closest to the truth.

A big part of the answer lies in being honest about our human subjectivity. On this side of heaven, in biblical terms, we all look "through a glass darkly"(1 Corinthians 13:12). We believe as the people of God that there can be creative and redemptive ways to face our many-storied and pluralistic stage in history. Walking down the pathway of honest self-definition will be a healthy beginning.

HONEST SELF-DEFINITION

God's truth is not relative, but it is subject to the cultural and personal biases we bring to our understanding of what is true. If we had the capacity to see as God sees and understand as God understands, then we could have a full and even a pure grasp of truth (Isaiah 55:8). However, our humanness precludes that possibility. Both consciously and unconsciously, we bring our cultural baggage and personal experiences to our understanding of the truth of the gospel.

Our perceptions and conclusions about the Christian faith are both filtered and influenced by our personal and church perspectives. To be blind or dishonest about these realities will mar our ability to communicate and incarnate the gospel of Jesus Christ in today's pluralistic world. Confessing one's biases and owning one's subjectivity does not undermine confidence in God's revealed truth. Rather, being truthful about our human limitations releases new levels of honesty that can reinforce our deep religious convictions, especially when they are touched with a godly sense of humility.

To own our biases is not to embrace relativism.

Speaking in Vancouver at a Regent College public lecture, scholar Edith Humphrey acknowledged the reality of relative certainty. Referring to the Jesus Seminar (where scholars judge the reliability of Jesus' sayings as they are recorded in Scripture) Humphrey reminded her evangelical audience, "The fact is, none of us simply reads the Bible. All of us, consciously or unconsciously, stand within a tradition of interpretation ... so doing history isn't an option. We do it either consciously or unconsciously, badly or well, just as we do theology."[5]

While recently teaching a group of clergy in the city of Nairobi, I [Gary] had to wrestle with the demands of affirming God's truth across cultures. The class included missionary leaders from Uganda and Kenya, as well as from several conservative evangelical denominations in the US and Canada. In that mix, participants were quickly able to identify the cultural baggage they brought to their understanding of God's truth. After working in cross cultural settings, they more easily understood how their own backgrounds had shaped their faith.

Whether in Canada or in Kenya, whatever our biases, we need to own how we construct our religious worldviews. Whether we embrace Catholic, Orthodox, mainline Protestant or evangelical faith perspectives, whether we are conservative or liberal, traditional or postmodern, we will have integrity when we are honest with ourselves and confessional with others.

To own our biases is not to embrace relativism. Being deliberate about confessing our biases gives us the right to tell our story. Identifying our way of understanding the truth allows us to be confident and content with our state of "relative certainty." As someone in our travels said, "To be honest, that's as much as we can claim. That's as good as it gets."

BE PREPARED TO EXCLUDE — EVENTUALLY

The very idea of "relative certainty" will sound like a "sell out" to some committed followers of Jesus. They will contend that "relativism has won and truth has lost." They will want to be more exclusive. Others will insist that even "relative certainty" still claims too much. They will argue, "You are still locked in the rational mode of enlightenment thinking." They will want to be more inclusive.

Some Christian voices will claim "their way is the only way." With their attitudes and actions, they endorse cultural fundamentalism. When pushed to conform by others, their natural inclination is to push back with equal force. Their strength is that they rarely give up any ground to others. Their weakness is that the only people they influence are those who already agree with them. Christians at the other extreme may be too ready to give up ground to others. They risk being culturally assimilated. Instead of being an influence for the reign of God in today's world, they get influenced by the prevailing ways of the world.

We propose a different strategy of dialogue with the world at large. This strategy flows from the New Testament church as it preached and demonstrated the gospel of Jesus Christ to a secular world in the first century. In the early days of New Testament church, Thomas was included in the community of faith even as he questioned the reality of the resurrected Christ in which the community found its identity. That same attitude of openness and acceptance is critical for effective communication of Christ's message in our day. A secure and healthy church invites dialogue and includes people who don't have it all together.

Still, the implications of the gospel cannot be avoided. Communities of faith must be ready to draw lines and take stands. The challenge to the church is to live with a spirit of inclusion, while also being ready to exclude if necessary.

Every Christian church has an obligation to self-define in at least two areas: belief and behavior. Beliefs are part of defining what it means to be Christian. Earlier in this chapter, we took a stand on the important issue of the uniqueness of Jesus Christ. Some distinctive behaviors and values also define Christian believers as the people of God. Just as sexual assault, bank robberies, and drug trafficking breach the criminal code, immorality, greed, and deliberate dishonesty contravene clear biblical Christian standards.

God forgives and grace abounds, but a perpetual disregard of God's directives amounts to the abuse of grace. Churches have boundaries. Eventually, those who do not live inside the boundaries define themselves as outsiders. They belong elsewhere. Episcopalian Robert Capon speaks to the issue.

The ordained ministry is not just a collection of Jacks and Jills who have been to seminary and, having gotten bravely over it, are now treasured for their skills as administrators, entertainers, amateur psychologists, and all purpose handy persons. They have a duty and a right to say what is and isn't Gospel – and they have a solemn obligation to tell the church it will have to drop dead to all such anti-Gospel nonsense if it really wants to live.[6]

A Buddhist priest, a friend of one of the authors, once asked, "All other religions exclude people. Why is it that Christians are so quick to give in to cultural pressures and accept things that are antithetical to the Christian faith?" We ask the same question.

Of course, the first impulse of Christian churches and their people must be to welcome others into their midst. The church channels the compassionate voice of Jesus, saying "come unto me." The God we worship loves, and commands us to share that love shared with others. The gift of Jesus' forgiveness is offered unconditionally to everyone.

But to pretend that the gift does not ask each person to make moral choices tokenizes and demeans the gift. Future Faith churches, like all churches who have a clear sense of who they are, struggle with the tension of being inclusive as well as being exclusive. They must be prepared to exclude – eventually.

Know WHERE We Are

Although churches with a clear identity have boundaries that sometimes exclude people, they are far more concerned about inviting and involving as many people as possible. One of the dispositions that enables them to advance is that they "know **where** they are." They are tuned into the environments around them. As they plan and orchestrate their ministry strategies, they are context specific.

ACCEPT GENERATIONAL DIFFERENCES

Future Faith churches attempt to see life from the other person's point of view. They are compassionate with the poor. They are more inclined to accept people than to judge them. Without being naïve, they grant the benefit of the doubt to people. This disposition extends to the younger generation, and in particular to Generation X, the generation that follows the Baby Boomers.

Generation gaps are not new. However, because church populations are older and younger Canadians in their 20s and early 30s are more inclined to opt out of church life than to be involved, giving attention to generational issues is crucial. The church's future is at stake. In the next 20 years, if the church is unable to attract and hold younger participants, it will be significantly smaller.

Researcher and demographer Michael Adams illustrates how generational differences affect how we think about families.

In Canada today, the model for "family values" has evolved from Leave it to Beaver *to* Murphy Brown. *In my parents' generation, rebellion was marriage between a Catholic and a Protestant, or a Protestant and a Jew. For my generation, the baby boomers, rebellion was common-law marriage, or divorce for those who did marry. For Generation X, rebellion is interracial unions, or the normalization of gay and lesbian relationships.*[7]

At our peril, we ignore these differences in the church. For the past six years, under the ministry umbrella of Inter-Varsity Christian Fellowship, over 600 students meet every Sunday evening in the pub of McMaster University. The highly energized music-oriented worship service is called "Church in the John." We would be wiser to take notice and learn from the venture's success than to criticize the venue. The younger generation is sending signals about what kind of spirituality will touch them and connect them with the Christian faith. Failing to understand and respond to the changing influences on generations will only produce negative results on the church's ministry. Proactively responding to generational concerns and interests will help us discover what computes the gospel into Good News for succeeding generations.

Responding to generational interests does not mean we need new churches or a specialized denomination. Rather, we need more listening to the heart cries of different age groups, so that we can provide places where like-minded people can hear each other and experience God. It will, however, demand changes in how we "do" church.

LOCAL CHURCHES WILL LEAD THEM

A spiritual and social trend is emerging across the nation. Local churches are becoming spotlights of spiritual vitality. They exist in every denomination. Anglican, Catholic, Pentecostal, Baptist, Presbyterian, Mennonite Brethren, Lutheran, or United – spiritually alive local churches are growing and leading the way for others in their denominations. Rather than expecting visions for a better future from brain trusts in church headquarters, God is raising up local churches as models of what others can become.

An intriguing dimension of the 14 churches we studied was that most of them felt somewhat marginalized within their denominations or religious traditions. The leaders expressed their struggle to find acceptance. They sometimes felt they had reputations as mavericks, or were considered to be dissonant voices within their church traditions.

Denominational loyalty is not a high value in today's world. People still prefer to stay with the denomination where they have personal history, but if they must choose between brand loyalty and a faith community that reflects their personal passions and values, denominational loyalty loses. One of the indicators of effectiveness of the Future Faith churches is their ability to thrive in this new environment. They are able to call people to a "grand story" that rallies people together around a bigger vision than themselves. Denominations will need to both appreciate and learn from these local congregations as they set the patterns for the next millennium.

> **Those who long for the good old days of denominational loyalty face a difficult future.**

Those who long for the good old days of denominational loyalty face a difficult future. Whatever the formal church governance may be, we can expect increased emotional intensity between denominational concerns and local church autonomy. In today's preference for personal choice, local churches have the first call on people's loyalty. Wise leaders of denominations will increasingly see themselves as resource providers to stimulate the effectiveness of local churches.

In the next stage of collective church life, headquarters personnel who assume roles as servants to empower local churches will help assure future denominational strength.

Know WHEN We Are

As we end this century and move beyond the year 2000, awareness of what is happening in the dominant culture will be crucial – whether the work of ministry is in local churches, para-church ministries, or in religious orders and seminaries. Without devaluing the role of the Holy Spirit or the important place of prayer, the claim still stands – doing ministry without understanding the culture is like walking into a dark room and not turning on the lights.

Harold Percy from Streetsville Anglican knows where the cultural light switch is located. He turns a spotlight on society and himself: "This culture is in captivity to idols, two of which are mammon and eros. I simply assume that everybody I deal with is in slavery to either money or sex or both – including myself half the time. It's a constant battle. They [mammon and eros] are so seductive you hardly even notice. They grab your imagination and capture your spirit. And if that's me – a guy who studied theology and biblical studies for seven or eight years, if that's the battle I fight – then pity the people who just walk in here from their workplaces trying to make sense out of life."

A CULTURE OF CHOICES

When we look at Canadian culture with the lights on, it is clear that modern living is like watching cable TV. People sit with channel changers in their hands, making choices and selecting preferences.

Particularly in the realm of beliefs and values and lifestyle alternatives, the dominant paradigm in Canadian life is, "I'll choose. I'll decide what to believe and how to behave." Self-determination is the preferred Canadian way. "I'll choose my educational path and where I want to live. I'll decide with whom I'll have sex, whether I'll marry or live in a common-law relationship, when to have children, and whether or not I stay with my partner." On the matter of morals, "I'll decide what is right and what is wrong, when to be honest and when to be dishonest."

On a societal scale, the pattern is the same. Instead of pressing for a greater consensus or seeking to build up the core culture, modern Canadian life champions individual choice.

Sometimes the fictitious world of television and the reality of life intersect. In the TV sitcom *Ellen*, the main character is played by Ellen DeGeneres, a self-confessed lesbian. Just prior to the program that revealed its star's lifestyle, *Entertainment Tonight* ran interviews with people from DeGeneres' hometown. The local pastor carefully expressed dissent for Ellen's lifestyle. An older woman was repulsed; she felt the program shouldn't be aired. A bearded young man stated the emerging cultural consensus to deify choice: "It's her choice – if that makes her happy, then people should be happy for her."[8]

American political philosopher Michael Sandall assesses the situation: "Our public life is rife with discontent." Sandall suggests two prominent symptoms of that discontent. He writes: "One is the fear that individually and collectively we are losing control of the forces that govern our lives and the other is the sense that, from family to neighborhood to nation, the moral fabric of community is unraveling around us."[9]

Canadian researcher Michael Adams is less alarmist. But he too points to changes in society that explain the increased fragmentation that is emerging around us. He observes that Canadians were once "defined by race, religion or region; now we define ourselves by our values, by our personal priorities, and by our life choices."[10]

Paradoxically, the value of making choices that fit with personal priorities ultimately feeds the appetite of individualism and pulls people away from values that nurture healthy communities and collective commitments. As a reader, you may or may not be happy about what is happening in the world that surrounds you. In this instance, however, there is no choice. In this moment in history, the "I'll decide – I'll choose" approach to life rules.

Living in a culture of choice does not mean God's committed people should passively surrender to everything in the society that surrounds them. Rather, when there is conflict between God's ways and the ways of the world, the church challenge is to call people to make choices that run counter to the culture. When "the way it is" in society shifts away from "what ought to be" in God's design for creation, serious Christians do not back away from making right choices.

Living in a culture of choice, they make decisions that are consistent with their personal convictions, which, over the long run, can lead to cultural corrections.

The current reality in these times is obvious, however. Encouraging and inspiring people to make right choices is far more strategic than attempting to take choices away from people.

CHURCH CHOICES

The same rules of life apply inside the church. Instead of resisting this culture of choice, wise church leaders will invite people to make positive choices. Rather than fearing choice as an instrument of individualism, innovative church leaders will offer choices to people as a strategy for involvement that leads to commitment and contribution. In the old church program paradigm, clergy and lay decision-makers expected people to involve themselves in whatever agenda the church offered. Often, they expected that everyone who was a part of the congregation would get involved in the same program at the same time. Involvement in church programs was the mark of commitment.

In the new church program paradigm, participants have choices. Certainly there is an expectation that the committed will attend worship regularly, but participation beyond worship is a matter of choice from a range of program alternatives.

The invitation to become a member of a small group is an example that illustrates the point. Small group gurus tend to conclude that small groups are good for *everyone*. Some new models of church ministry *require* small group participation. In churches that promote involvement in cell groups or small groups, people are likely to hear announcements like, "If you really desire to be a part of this church, you will be an active member of the small group that meets in your neighborhood."

A wiser strategy would state the priority as a choice: "Being involved in a small group is one important way for you to participate in the spiritual life of your church." Even when a local church determines that small groups are central to their model, a maximum of 50% of the total number of parishioners will ever get involved. Put another way, no more than half the people will get involved – even if small groups are the church's primary program. Small groups are not for everyone.

Wise church leaders will invite people to make positive choices.

In recent research conducted by the Angus Reid Group, a representative sample of Canadians who were regular church attenders were asked: "Are you part of a small group in your church, such as a service group, Bible study, or discussion group?"

SMALL GROUP INVOLVEMENT

Church attendance	% involved in small groups
Weekly	43%
Monthly	12%
Few times a year	2%

Source: Angus Reid Group, National Survey, June 1994; Total sample size: 1500

People who attend church on a weekly basis are also those who are most probable to join a small group. In the main, small groups are a second choice commitment for those who are already involved.

Another predictable factor is that some denominations are more likely to attract people into small groups than others.

SMALL GROUP ATTENDERS BY DENOMINATION

	% who attend weekly
Evangelical Protestant	56
Mainline Protestant	50
Catholic	31

Source: as in page 213

We live in a culture of choice. In Canadian life, people expect the privilege of exercising their personal prerogatives. The people who come to church bring those assumptions with them. They expect to make choices in church too. Instead of lamenting the situation, church decision-makers "who know **when** they are" will gladly affirm that the God they desire to serve placed the privilege and responsibility of choice into the order of creation. They will invite people within the range of their influence to make positive choices.

MAKE PEACE WITH CULTURAL PLURALISM
A recent discussion is etched in my [Don's] mind. The conversation followed a presentation which wrestled with how to be serious Christians while relating in positive ways to others who live differently.

After the session, an older woman approached me. She had been a missionary in India for 40 years. In India, she said, "There were demands on my time, there were opportunities to serve and to accomplish what I believe were significant things for God and people." Then she paused and said, "The Canada I've returned to is different from the Canada I left." Another moment of silence passed before she continued, "Now I have time and I have this desire to witness and care for people, but I'm confused. I don't know how any more."

In the opinion of your authors, figuring out how to live faithfully as followers of Jesus in modern Canada will include making peace with cultural pluralism. The appeal to live peaceably and productively with cultural pluralism is quite different from cuddling up to relativism or passively accommodating to increasing secularization.

Relativism as an ideology denies the possibility of truth. According to relativism, the only claim Christianity can make is that it is one view of life among many other views. Secularism also contradicts what the Christian faith affirms. As a belief system, secularism constructs life without any need for God and, in the end, is an enemy of the Christian faith.

In contrast, "cultural pluralism invites people in a single society who believe different things to live peaceably and productively alongside each other." In support of diversity in a society, a healthy and principled cultural pluralism calls for attitudes that both accept and affirm our differences by creating "social structures for cradling diversity."[11]

If our cultural pluralism in Canada can mature, it will not just be a protector of various minority voices in our society, it will also be a friend of the faith. Because cultural pluralism is mandated to make room for diversity, it is also obligated to make room for the many expressions of the Christian faith that are espoused by the diversity of churches across the land. Because church-attending Christians are now a distinct minority group within the broader culture, it will be to their advantage to make cultural pluralism work.

With insight and clarity, Roman Catholic theologian Hervé Carrier describes the difference between how people came to faith in the past compared to the challenges churches face in today's pluralistic society:

In the past, cultures and institutions became Christian not so much through a specific strategy as through the slow penetration of Christ's teaching into lifestyles and social structures. Today, the capillary spread of Gospel values into the social fabric is blocked because of the wide gap existing between the Christian faith and the prevailing ethos of the industrialized world. Announcing Jesus Christ to modern minds calls for a profound revision of traditional methods of evangelization.[12]

Making peace with cultural pluralism is one of the necessary revisions the modern church must negotiate. For Catholics and mainline Protestants, hanging on to the assumptions of Christendom are futile. The age of cultural privilege and special status for the church is over. For evangelicals, plotting adversarial strategies to will their way on the majority will fail. The will and ways of the dominant culture will not be swayed by loud voices or court interventions. The more redemptive way is to focus on reality and chart a strategy for effectiveness that will also be spiritually faithful. The following list is offered as a beginning step into what can be a fruitful future.

TEN COMMANDMENTS FOR CULTURAL PLURALISM

1. Know who you are, what you believe, and then be true to yourself
2. Grant others the same prerogative to self-define and be true to themselves
3. Yield not to the temptation of denigrating those who are different from self
4. Extend to others the same rights and privileges you desire for yourself

---

5. Invite others to make positive choices about their beliefs and behaviors
6. Protect those who are not positioned to protect themselves
7. Lobby in life for God's ways of justice and what enhances the common good
8. Treat others the way you would like to be treated
9. Expect others to treat you the way you treat them
10. Treat people the way God treats people, and let God take care of judging of others

As Christians living in a pluralistic society, we can be clear voices for Christ. We can live without compromise and be true to ourselves. However, we must acknowledge that the Christian voice is not the only view in our multi-voiced society. The best overall strategy in relating and living with regard for others is to practice the golden rule: "In everything do to others as you would have them do to you"(Matthew 7:22).

The biggest challenge is to express the Christian alternative so that it becomes the preferred choice among other cultural choices.

EMBRACE CONVICTION AND COMPASSION

One difficulty of living faithfully in these times is that we have not had a lot of practice in dealing with diversity. We remember when life's arithmetic was simpler: one career, one marriage, one model of family, one dominant religion. We feel new tensions as we seek to honor our own beliefs while still extending respect to others who live differently.

One helpful response to the tension is to embrace the double strengths of conviction and compassion. **Conviction** invites us to self-define and incorporate into our essence what we believe God is asking from us. **Compassion** sensitizes us to the value of others and the specific circumstances of their lives.

One way to envision the dynamics of conviction and compassion is to see them as guard rails that keep us on the road of faith. Like other highways, the road of faith has ditches on both sides. We can slide into excesses. The guard rails protect us from swerving off the road. The guard rail of conviction is protection for ourselves. We are kept from becoming passive and spineless, uncertain and permissive. The guard rail of compassion protects our relationship with others. We are kept from being judgmental and intolerant, arrogant and rude.

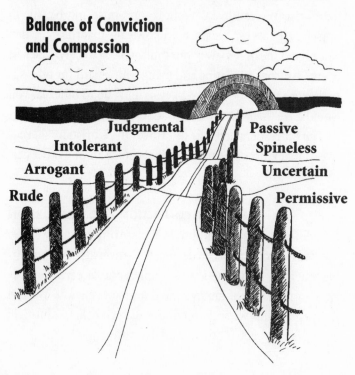

Balance of Conviction and Compassion

Judgmental
Intolerant
Arrogant
Rude

Passive
Spineless
Uncertain
Permissive

Particularly in these pluralistic times, a benefit of living with clear convictions is that we are freed to relate to others who put life together in different ways. Author William Blair Gould insightfully points out, "The more weakly we stand on the ground of our belief ... the more we cling with both hands to the dogma which separates it from other beliefs; on the other hand, the more firmly we stand on the ground of our faith, the more we have both hands free to reach out to others who cannot share our belief."[13]

Calling for compassion toward people who embrace other world religions, Archbishop of Canterbury George Carey offered wise Christian counsel in a news report. Mere tolerance between the faiths was not enough, he said. He called for "friendship, not hostility; understanding, not ignorance; reciprocity, not exclusivism; and cooperation, not confrontation."[14]

Following a public gathering where I [Don] had been the speaker, a broad shouldered older man with a peaceful face reached out to shake my hand. I couldn't help but notice that his hand felt like coarse sandpaper. His first words were, "I work with wood." In that moment, my mind made the connection to the speech I had just delivered where I had quoted Dorothy Sayers and her vocational tribute to Jesus as a carpenter: "No crooked table-legs or ill fitting drawers ever, I dare swear, came out of the carpenter's shop at Nazareth."[15]

The gentle man who continued to hold my hand would not win an award for small talk. His words were precise. "I prefer to work with mahogany," he said. "Mahogany is soft and pliable. Mahogany is forgiving. Not like oak. Oak is hard and inflexible. There is no room for mistakes when you are working with oak. Mahogany is what I like to work with." Without any further conversation, he smiled, released my hand, and walked toward the exit.

The people and leaders in Future Faith churches are more like mahogany than oak. They are not inflexible or harsh. They are strong enough to be forgiving. They know in their own journeys that they sometimes jump the guard rails and travel in the ditch. Consequently, they are pliable and ready to extend compassion in their relationships with others. But they are not ready to bend to the point of breaking. They treasure their relationship with God too much, and their convictions are too well-established to be easily disregarded.

Continually Practice a Two-Edged Faith

Churches are meant to be more like manufacturing plants than advertising agencies. Manufacturing plants produce products; advertising agencies simply sell the products the manufacturing plants produce. General Motors and Chrysler Corporation produce automobiles at the end of their assembly lines. IBM and Toshiba plants manufacture computers. Furniture factories build furniture. If any of these stop producing products, they cease to exist.

Healthy churches energized by the Spirit of God produce spiritually transformed people – people who love God and have compassion for others.

KNOW GOD AND LOVE JESUS

If churches are going to be spiritually transforming places, church leaders need to be certain that they address and resolve one particular matter. Whatever the denomination or religious tradition, whether the worship style is highly liturgical or free spirited and spontaneous, the issue is same: how do people in particular church traditions experience the personal touch of God? In what ways do people encounter Jesus in a personal way and nurture their relationship in Christ?

This concern is not an attempt to control how God's spirit works in faith communities and in the lives of people. After all, "the wind blows where it will" (John 3:8). Rather, it is a concern that church leaders be intentional about inviting people to get in touch with God, to taste the presence of God, and to experience forgiveness in Christ.

Healthy churches produce spiritually transformed people – people who love God and have compassion for others.

Understanding the Christian life as an invitation into a relationship with Christ is accepted widely as a basic Christian understanding. The idea that the divine presence is present in Christian believers, that we can know God exists because we experience God, and that the Holy Spirit abides in the spirit of Christian believers, is central to our faith.

As evangelical spokesperson Philip Yancey asks: "On our own, would any of us come up with the notion of a God who loves and yearns to be loved?"[16] Yancey images the biblical story as God's "rescue plan of love. In a nutshell, the Bible from Genesis 3 to Revelation 22 tells the story of a God reckless with desire to get his family back" in a restored relationship of love.[17]

Catholic theologian Karl Rahner is convinced that the mystical dimension has to be the future focus of Christian life and spirituality: "A religion perceived as grounded in propositions and dogmas is not enough to sustain today's Christian," he writes. "Without an awareness of the depth dimension they will lose faith and fade away, as many have already done."[18]

Marcus Borg, a self-confessed liberal, frames his theology within his personal experience of faith: "Until my late thirties, I saw the Christian life as being primarily about believing. Like many of us, as a child I had no problem with belief. But at the end of childhood I struggled with doubt and disbelief. All through this period I continued to think that believing was what the Christian life was all about … Now I no longer see the Christian life as being primarily about believing … Rather it is giving one's heart to Jesus … It is the movement from secondhand religion to firsthand religion, from having heard about Jesus with the hearing of the ear to being in relationship with the Spirit of Christ."[19]

After studying mainline churches in the US, Hadaway and Roozen came to the same conclusion: "Churches whose primary concern is making people full of God are also churches whose pews will be full of people."[20] Future Faith churches invite people to enter a relationship with Jesus Christ and experience the living God.

MOTIVATE SOCIAL COMPASSION

In God's design for the church, spiritually transformed people are meant to contribute to the social transformation of society. What other conclusion can come out of the meaning of the Great Command? People who love God are also to love their neighbors. In other words, those who are spiritually transformed by loving God and being loved by God, are in turn to socially transform their neighbors in need by loving and caring for them.

Mark Noll, a historian from Wheaton College, confesses, "In general responses to crises, evangelicals in the late 20th century still follow a pathway defined at the start of the 20th century. When faced with a crisis situation, we evangelicals usually do one of two things. We either mount a public crusade, or we retreat into an inner pious sanctum."[21] Even prayer can be a tranquilizer for doing nothing – well-intentioned, but still a form of cheap charity. Public crusades are much more effective when Christian leaders are able to go to governments and augment their calls for change with evidence showing that, "We are part of Christian communities that are already beginning to live out what we are calling you to legislate."[22]

The evangelical voice of N.T. Wright affirms the same theme and reasserts the social care agenda. What we need is a real Jesus, says Wright – "Jesus as the gospels give him to us: the Jesus of the Galilean lanes and villages, the Jesus who called Herod 'that fox,' the Jesus whose practical agenda rang so many disturbing bells in first-century Palestine – bells which are so neatly silenced when we transplant him out of that context."[23]

As an influential evangelical and long time advocate of the poor, Ron Sider's commitment to both sides of the faith equation is evident: "If we understand and practice genuinely biblical repentance, then we establish an important, inseparable link between conversion and Christian social responsibility. Biblical repentance includes turning from all sin, including social sins."[24] The respected voice of J. Howard Yoder agrees and mandates social action which includes a call for the church to be involved in advocacy that addresses systemic causes: "To follow Jesus does not mean ... sacrificing concern for liberation within the social process in favor of delayed gratification in heaven, or abandoning efficacy in favor of purity."[25] Catholic spokesperson Hervé Carrier's insight adds further clarity: "Evangelization remains unfinished if it does not achieve justice and transform cultures."[26]

It is only honest to acknowledge that Future Faith churches are much more involved in compassionate community ministries than they are in addressing systemic causes of injustice. Their journeys of social care are worthy of emulating, but they still have distances to travel. Nevertheless, they are leading the way. Future Faith churches "do not retreat from their responsibilities as members of society; quite the opposite. They take their place in the tradition of Moses, Amos, Hosea, Isaiah, Micah, Jeremiah, Mary, James, and John the Baptist."[27]

Graduate student and research assistant for this project Daryl Thomson states it right: "A place can be found for faith and action to join hands and serve in unity." This research decisively concludes that Future Faith churches are places where faith and action are connected; where dynamic personal faith and active social concern are integral parts of each other; where soul care and social care are fused together.

The visual graphic on the next page reveals the results of a statistical analysis of the Future Faith churches in the research project. Using a factor analysis methodology, all of the churches cluster together in the "high soul care – high social care" quadrant. The primary input for the analysis utilized the 21 statements from item #7 in the survey (printed in Appendix 7). Asked to identify the present practices of their church, the 418 survey respondents confirmed the story we have been telling. Future Faith churches are "love God and love your neighbor" people. The essence of the Christian life includes both soul care and social care.

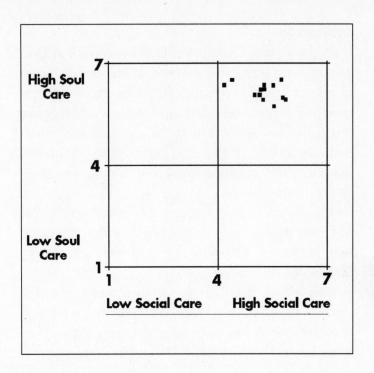

SOUL CARE AND SOCIAL CARE

Soul Care Emphases	Social Care Emphases
Day to day application of faith	Community service
Biblical command "to love God and your neighbor as yourself"	Help Canadians living in poverty Programs out in the community
Personal devotional life	Service with deeds
Importance of truth	Importance of social action
Development of personal faith	Correcting injustices in society[28]

CONCLUSION

On a global scale, two individuals, both anointed by God, have emerged as the "patron saints" of soul care and social care. For the past 25 years, their faces have graced magazine covers. They have been featured TV guests on high profile programs. They received front page news coverage wherever they traveled. They are revered by Christians around the world. They are respected by people who have little or no regard for God.

The "patron saint" of soul care is Billy Graham. The patron saint of social care is Mother Teresa. Mother Teresa and Billy Graham have each gifted the church and the world with their faithfulness and excellence.

Both "patron saints" are now in their sunset years. The news coverage they attract today centers more on their personal health than the continued effectiveness of their ministries. Neither Billy Graham nor Mother Teresa would separate their grasp of the gospel into the separated streams of "soul" and "social," but each legacy does have a dominant theme. They epitomize the best of what God has called them to pursue.

Future Faith churches are gifting the body of Christ with a vision that lifts up both sides of the gospel equation at the same time. In their pursuit of ministry that champions both a love for God and compassion for people, they are leading edge churches for the 21st century. As faith communities, they are also full-fledged biblical people.

The Scriptures call the church and the people of God everywhere to soul care.

So if anyone is in Christ, there is a new creation: everything old has passed away; see, everything has become new! All this is

*from God, who reconciled us to himself through Christ, and has
given us the ministry of reconciliation. (2 Corinthians 5:17-18)*

The Scriptures call the church and the people of God everywhere to social care.

*We know love by this, that he laid down his life for us and we
ought to lay down our lives for one another. How does God's
love abide in anyone who has the world's goods and sees a brother
or sister in need and yet refuses help? Let us love, not in word or
speech, but in truth and action. (1 John 3:16-18).*

When soul care and social care are fused together, the church
is the church and the people of God are the people of God.

APPENDICES

Appendix 1

FUTURE FAITH CHURCHES

Rev David Watt
First Baptist Church
100 Ochterloney
Dartmouth NS B2Y 3Y3

Rev Barry Parker
St John's the Evangelist Anglican
1111 57th Ave.
Edmonton AB T6H 0Z6

Pastor Paul Wartman
The Meeting Place
139 Smith St.
Winnipeg MB R3C 1J5

Rev Doug Ward
Kanata Baptist Church
465 Hazeldean Rd.
Kanata ON K2L 1V1

Rev Carlin Weinhauer
Willingdon M.B. Church
4812 Willingdon Ave
Vancouver BC V5G 3H6

Rev Tim Dickau
Grandview Calvary Church
1803 East 1st Ave.
Vancouver BC V5N 1B2

Dr. Terry Ingram
Oakridge Presbyterian Church
862 Freele St.
London ON N6H 3P3

Rev Harold Percy
Trinity Church Streetsville
69 Queen St. South
Mississauga ON L5M 1K5

Rev Mike Rietsma
First Christian
Reformed Church
3600 15A Street S.W.
Calgary AB T2T 5P8

Rev Jennifer Ferguson
Rev John Pentland
Deer Park United Church
77 Deer Point Rd. S.E.
Calgary AB T2J 6W5

Pastor Warren Lai
Scarborough Chinese
Baptist Church
2610 Birchmount Rd.
Scarborough ON M1W 2P5

Father Corbin Eddy
Saint Basil's RC Church
940 Rex Ave.
Ottawa ON K2A 2P7

Pastor Wesley Campbell
New Life Vineyard Fellowhip
2041 Harvey Ave.
Kelowna BC V1Y 6G7

Pastor Daniel Doolittle
Six Nations
Pentecostal Church
Box 10, 4th Line
Oshweken ON N0A 1M0

Appendix 2

RESEARCH PROJECT METHODOLOGY

PURPOSE

To identify and analyze a cross section of effective churches in Canada that have a holistic understanding of the gospel and are motivating their people to pursue the Great Command, both to love God and to love their neighbors.

RESEARCH DESIGN

The sample of 14 churches listed in Appendix 1 was selected, not to generalize to the larger church-attending population, but to analyze and profile churches as defined by the purpose. Purposive or judgmental samples consist of elements (respondents, cases, time segments, etc.) deliberately chosen or hand-picked for a study's purposes. Accordingly, cases may be selected for inclusion because they are thought to be typical of what one is interested in studying. (William J. Reid and Audrey D. Smith, *Research in Social Work,* New York: Columbia University Press, 1989, 180.)

CHURCH SELECTION PROCESS

A total of 425 nomination requests were mailed to a representative sample of World Vision Canada's *Context* readership list. The response resulted in 302 nominations, including 27 churches from 8 different denominations that received multiple nominations. The nomination form with the stated criteria is included in Appendix 3.

FOCUS GROUP AND LEADERSHIP INTERVIEWS

The discussion and interview guides are printed in Appendix 4 & 5. The qualitative data was thematically organized and analyzed using the computer program SQR NUD*IST (Non-numerical Unstructured Data Indexing and Searching and Theorizing).

QUESTIONNAIRE RESPONSE

(Questionnaire printed in Appendix 7)
Distribution: 50 surveys at each of the 14 churches: N:700
Total returned: 418 from 13 churches
Response Rate: 60%
Demographic data of respondents: Gender: Female = 52%   Male = 48%
Age: less than 18 = 2%   19-24 = 5%   25-34 = 16%   35-44 = 28%   45-54 = 23%   55-64 = 12%   More than 65 = 14%
Roles: Clergy = 10%   Lay Leaders = 30%   Lay Attenders = 60%

NOTES OF INTEREST

- 49% had been attending the same church for at least 8 consecutive years
- 51% had stopped attending church at some time in their lives
- 23% had stopped attending any church for between 5-10 years
- 10% of the sample had "no religious background"
- Focus group and leadership interviews were transcribed into files totaling over 700 pages of text.

Appendix 3

GUIDELINES
FOR IDENTIFYING CHURCHES
in your denomination/religious tradition
pursuing full-fledged faith

Here's the research dilemma. Over-definition tends to prede-termine results ... Under-definition generates ambiguity. Ac-cordingly, three criteria are offered to help identify these churches – Quality, Quantity, and Balance.

QUALITY: THE CHURCH EVIDENCES
SPIRITUAL VITAL SIGNS
In ways that are compatible with the church's style and tradi-tion, participants deepen their lives in Christ. The great com-mand to love and the great commission to make disciples are on the church's agenda. Churches are not just landlords to house social activities but their people are personally involved in the practice of their faith ... Spiritual needs are met and direction for living in the modern world is provided. Devo-tion to God is nurtured. GOD IS PRESENT.

QUANTITY: INCREASING NUMBERS OF PEOPLE
ARE GETTING INVOLVED
Effective and successful churches grow. More people partici-pate. Or in some situations, the circumstances that would normally result in a decline are countered and a church keeps their numerical balance while nurturing qualitative growth. Church growth is not the total picture of an effective church but involving increasing numbers of people is a sign of a healthy church.

BALANCED FAITH: CHURCH TEACHING AND
PROGRAMMING ARE INTENTIONALLY HOLISTIC

Healthy worship is experienced, learning that is linked to life is evident, serving those who have needs is an active concern, and people are encouraged to share their faith. Personal faith is celebrated and a concern for social justice is expressed.

Obviously, there are no perfect churches – but across the country and in our different denominations and various religious traditions there are churches pursuing and practicing full-fledged faith.

Let's find them, affirm them and learn from them. Thanks again ...

Appendix 4

GUIDELINES FOR SELECTING FOCUS GROUP PARTICIPANTS

Governing Principle: To gather a representative sample (a cross section) of people who attend your church on a regular (weekly & at least a couple times a month) basis.

Size of group: Not less than 7, not more than 10. (Please confirm at least 8 or 9 to allow for last minute cancellations)

Representation: Give consideration to ...
• Age
• Gender
• Ethnicity (if applicable)
• Family structure diversity (divorced/remarried, single etc.)
• Years of involvement
• Varied levels of involvement (e.g., formal leaders/program and structure, at least one Sunday-morning-only attender)

Note: Complete representation is impossible. You will want to choose people who have a sense of your church's understanding of the gospel and vision for ministry.

Appendix 5

FOCUS GROUP INSTRUMENT

INTRODUCTION

Your church has been nominated by others as an effective church in today's society. Not perfect, but it is perceived by others to be a healthy church ... positive for people to be involved in ...

Sketch outline of what will be covered ... state time limit ...

PROPOSED QUESTIONS

1. Sketch scenario – Someone you know asks you about your church ...
   Complete statement: "What I like about our church is
   _____."
   (Discuss among participants or write three responses)

2. If circumstances changed so that you could no longer attend this church, what would you miss the most?

3. What does your church emphasize about the Christian faith? In other words, how does your church help people understand the Bible's teachings and what it means to be faithful to Christ?

4. Tell me how your church helps people. Have a closer relationship with God? Live as Christians in their daily lives – outside the church?

236 • FUTURE FAITH CHURCHES

5. How does your church address problems in this community among people in need?

6. Think about the future – complete the statements: "I would be extremely disappointed with our church if
_____."

7. "I think our church should _____."
How has involvement in this church affected you – changed your life?

Appendix 6

LEADERSHIP INTERVIEW GUIDE

1. Ministry history/church history/personal history
- What was the church like when you first arrived?
- Compared to when you began, what is different about this church today?
- Have there been some major events, struggles, moments of breakthrough?

2. Complete the statement:
- "What I like about our church is ..."

3. Philosophy of ministry
- What is your philosophy of ministry? What theological/ministry themes frame your church emphasis?
- How have you tried to implement your philosophy and vision (or these themes/emphases) into the life of this church?

If the response does not include the personal and the social, ask:
- How do you help people in this church:
  – Have a closer relationship with God?
  – Live as Christians in their daily lives, outside the church?
- How does your church address problems in this community among people in need?

4. Leadership style
- How do you think people in your church describe your leadership style?
- Are you satisfied with your leadership style or would you like to change it? If so, how?

5. Coping with change
- Today's world is changing; dealing with change is inescapable. How are you helping your people deal with changes in society?
- Thinking about the dynamics of change inside the church, what reflections do you have about the process of organizational change?

6. Source of influence and inspiration
- What have been the primary sources of influence and inspiration that have shaped your ministry?
- When you reflect on the future of the church, where do you tend to look for strategic direction?

7. Briefly complete three statements:
- "When I think about my ministry here, my greatest satisfaction comes from _____."
- "I would be extremely disappointed with our church if _____."
- "I think our church should _____."

8. Achievements
- If you were to propose a toast or offer a tribute to what you consider to be the most significant achievement of this church in the past five years, what would you would say?

Appendix 7

EFFECTIVE CHURCH SURVEY

Your church has been nominated by others as an effective church in today's society. Not perfect, but it is perceived by others to be a healthy church ... purposeful and positive for people to be involved in.

This research project is sponsored by World Vision Canada. Desiring to be a responsible partner with the church in Canada and knowing that there are social segments of poverty inside our borders, several years ago World Vision initiated a National Programs department. Today, NeighbourLink is mobilizing church attending Christians to respond to people in their communities who have specific needs, refugees are being assisted to become contributing Canadians and there are new ministry initiatives among our Aboriginal Peoples. In addition, clergy and lay decision-makers are using World Vision's research as a means to understand the place of the church in contemporary society.

You may have heard that your minister has already been interviewed and that a focus group from your congregation has met to share the inside story of your church. In October 1997, national PRAXIS Conferences will profile the results of the research. The strategy will invite others to learn from the experiences of healthy and vibrant churches. Along with others, your responses will help write the script of what a preferred future can look like.

Thank you for your participation and contribution.

1. The following statements relate to personal religious beliefs. No matter how you answer the questions, you can be sure that many people feel the same way. Please indicate the extent to which you agree or disagree with the following statements. (Circle the number which best represents your personal opinion)

1	2	3	4
Strongly Agree	Agree	Disagree	Strongly Disagree

I believe the Bible is the inspired word of God	1	2	3	4
I don't think you need to go to church to be a good Christian	1	2	3	4
I consider myself to be a converted Christian	1	2	3	4
I feel it is very important to encourage non-Christians to become Christians	1	2	3	4
All the great religions of the world are equally good and true	1	2	3	4
My private beliefs about Christianity are more important than what is taught by any church	1	2	3	4
I usually experience God's presence at a worship service	1	2	3	4
Churches and religious organizations should spend more money on helping the poor	1	2	3	4
Christianity is only one route to salvation	1	2	3	4
My religious faith is very important to me in my day-to-day life	1	2	3	4

2. Next, consider the following statements people make about some political and social issues.

1	2	3	4
Strongly Agree	Agree	Disagree	Strongly Disagree

Christians should get involved in politics	1	2	3	4
Christians should get involved in politics to use their influence to advance their values	1	2	3	4
It is essential that traditional Christian values play a major role in Canadian politics	1	2	3	4
If I had my choice, I would rather have next door neighbors who are my own color	1	2	3	4
The number of immigrants who can legally enter Canada should be reduced	1	2	3	4
The government should spend more to fight hunger and poverty even if it means higher taxes	1	2	3	4
The gap between the rich and poor in this country is a significant problem	1	2	3	4
It is best not to get too involved in taking care of other people's needs	1	2	3	4

3. Please indicate if you agree or disagree, strongly or moderately, with the following statements:

1	2	3	4
Strongly Agree	Agree	Disagree	Strongly Disagree

Most people are poor because they don't work hard enough to get ahead in this world	1	2	3	4
I would be prepared to pay higher taxes so the government could do more for poor people in developing countries	1	2	3	4
Even in these difficult economic times, our government should maintain its current levels of aid to developing countries in the third world	1	2	3	4
I feel I personally have an important responsibility to help people in poor countries around the world	1	2	3	4
Because of government cutbacks, I feel there is the need for charities and other groups to help the poor and needy in our society	1	2	3	4
Most of the aid sent to poorer countries never gets to those who need it most	1	2	3	4
Poverty and homelessness is a growing problem in this country	1	2	3	4

4. Other than on special occasions such as weddings, funerals, or baptisms, how often did you attend religious services or meetings in the last 12 months ? Was it ? (Mark your response)

- ❑ More than once a week
- ❑ Once a week
- ❑ A few times a month
- ❑ Once a month
- ❑ A few times a year
- ❑ At least once a year

I am a formal member of this church
- ❑ Yes   ❑ No

5. The Christian life is expressed both inside and outside the church. How often do you ...

1	2	3	4	5
Once a day or more	Once a week or more	Once a month or more	Occasionally	Never

	1	2	3	4	5
Pray outside of formal religious services?	1	2	3	4	5
Read the Bible or other religious material outside of church?	1	2	3	4	5
Talk to others who do not attend church about spiritual matters?	1	2	3	4	5
Watch religious television?	1	2	3	4	5
Regularly participate in a small group (Bible study, prayer, service, etc.)	1	2	3	4	5

6. Generally speaking, do you think that your church is giving adequate direction in the following areas? Circle either "yes" or "no".

Making moral decisions in today's society	Yes	No
The problems of family life	Yes	No
People's personal spiritual needs	Yes	No
The social problems facing our country today	Yes	No
Living as a Christian in the workplace	Yes	No
Practical ways to respond to community needs	Yes	No

7. Various churches concentrate on different aspects of the Christian faith.

For each item below, please circle the number that indicates the emphasis your church places on various aspects of the Christian life.

Make your choices thinking about the present practices of the church you attend. Think about completing the sentence, "My church emphasizes ..."

1	2	3	4	5		6		7	
Unimportant			Somewhat Important					Very Important	

Outreach to others	1	2	3	4	5	6	7
Building parish\congregational life	1	2	3	4	5	6	7
Community service	1	2	3	4	5	6	7
Congregational growth	1	2	3	4	5	6	7
Missions within Canada	1	2	3	4	5	6	7
Biblical command "to go into the world and make disciples"	1	2	3	4	5	6	7
Witnessing with words	1	2	3	4	5	6	7
Service with deeds	1	2	3	4	5	6	7
Evangelism	1	2	3	4	5	6	7
Biblical command "to love God and your neighbour as yourself"	1	2	3	4	5	6	7
Help Canadians living in poverty	1	2	3	4	5	6	7
Day to day application of faith	1	2	3	4	5	6	7
Social action	1	2	3	4	5	6	7
Personal devotional life	1	2	3	4	5	6	7
Importance of truth	1	2	3	4	5	6	7
Development of personal faith	1	2	3	4	5	6	7
Help people living in poverty overseas	1	2	3	4	5	6	7
Programs inside the church	1	2	3	4	5	6	7
Missions outside Canada	1	2	3	4	5	6	7
Programs out in the community	1	2	3	4	5	6	7
Correcting injustice in society	1	2	3	4	5	6	7

8. What do you believe about the following statements? (Circle your response)

1	2	3	4
Strongly Agree	Agree	Disagree	Strongly Disagree

	1	2	3	4
I think effective churches are more likely than other churches to be open about addressing social problems from the pulpit such as domestic violence, child abuse, racism and alcoholism	1	2	3	4
I think churches should take a clear stand on issues like homosexuality, abortion and euthanasia	1	2	3	4
I think effective churches give equal status and leadership opportunities to men and women	1	2	3	4
In the future, I think Christianity and churches will increase their influence on Canadian life	1	2	3	4

9. God uses different people with different gifts in unique ways. There are many different leadership styles. And leadership styles can be categorized in numerous ways. Identify what you perceive to be the primary leadership style that best describes how the senior pastor or main ministers of your church tend to lead. Respond to each style cited:

1	2	3	4
Most Often	Often	Sometimes	Almost Never

	1	2	3	4
PERSUADE (Convince others to accept his/her ideas)	1	2	3	4
CONSULT (Share decision-making)	1	2	3	4
ENABLE (Equip the laity to perform ministry)	1	2	3	4
CONTROL (Needs to be in charge of everything)	1	2	3	4
DELEGATE (Hand over to others but with accountability)	1	2	3	4
ASSIGN (Give away with full responsibility)	1	2	3	4
INSPIRE (Motivate with enthusiasm and vision)	1	2	3	4

10. As I understand the role of leadership, when it comes to helping create a spiritually alive and effective church, I am in favour of ...

1	2	3	4
Strongly Agree	Agree	Disagree	Strongly Disagree

	1	2	3	4
Clergy leadership that stresses the leaders authority	1	2	3	4
Clergy leadership that is venturesome and inclined to take risks	1	2	3	4
Clergy leadership that seeks to gain the consensus of the church members before acting	1	2	3	4
Clergy leadership that is committed to the tasks of the church whether people are ready to follow or not	1	2	3	4
Clergy leadership that places a high priority on numerical growth	1	2	3	4
Clergy leadership that encourages church members to develop their gifts to serve and lead	1	2	3	4
Clergy leadership that leads with the strength of their personalities	1	2	3	4

11. Please indicate if you agree or disagree, strongly or moderately with the following statements:

1	2	3	4
Strongly Agree	Agree	Disagree	Strongly Disagree

	1	2	3	4
Most people can't be trusted	1	2	3	4
I feel it is best to trust people, even if they sometimes betray your trust	1	2	3	4
Donating time to volunteer organizations would be a waste of my time	1	2	3	4
I do volunteer work on a regular basis	1	2	3	4
I feel it is important to be very involved in the community you live in	1	2	3	4
What is right and wrong is a matter of personal opinion	1	2	3	4
I think you should keep you ideas of what is right and what is wrong to yourself	1	2	3	4
When I put my trust in other people they usually disappoint me	1	2	3	4
Doing good things for others can earn people a place in heaven	1	2	3	4

12. How important are the following church activities/functions for you?

1	2	3	4	5		6		7
Unimportant			Somewhat Important					Very Important

Good sermons	1	2	3	4	5	6	7
Bible studies	1	2	3	4	5	6	7
Social events at church	1	2	3	4	5	6	7
Activities for young people	1	2	3	4	5	6	7
Worshipping regularly	1	2	3	4	5	6	7
Church friends	1	2	3	4	5	6	7
A church for the family	1	2	3	4	5	6	7
Playing some role in the church	1	2	3	4	5	6	7
Good music	1	2	3	4	5	6	7
Efforts to influence society	1	2	3	4	5	6	7
Serving people in the community who have needs	1	2	3	4	5	6	7
A good Sunday school	1	2	3	4	5	6	7
Preparing for my Christian witness in the world	1	2	3	4	5	6	7
Small group involvement	1	2	3	4	5	6	7
Prayer groups	1	2	3	4	5	6	7

13. How important to YOUR FAITH are the following:

1	2	3	4	5		6		7
Unimportant			Somewhat Important					Very Important

Attending worship services	1	2	3	4	5	6	7
Being involved in the church	1	2	3	4	5	6	7
Caring about other people	1	2	3	4	5	6	7
Being ethical	1	2	3	4	5	6	7
Pursuing justice	1	2	3	4	5	6	7
Being concerned about the environment	1	2	3	4	5	6	7
Developing strong beliefs	1	2	3	4	5	6	7
Having a relationship with God	1	2	3	4	5	6	7
Responding to needs in my community	1	2	3	4	5	6	7
Confessing Jesus as Saviour and Lord	1	2	3	4	5	6	7
Sharing your faith with others	1	2	3	4	5	6	7
Learning how to think about issues in a distinct Christian way	1	2	3	4	5	6	7

This last section includes some questions about the church you attend and about yourself.

1. Which of the following best describes your position or area of involvement in the church you currently attend?
   - ❏ Minister/Pastor/Priest
   - ❏ Lay leader (board member, deacon, elder, etc)
   - ❏ Other clergy on multiple church staff
   - ❏ Lay attender

2. I participated in a focus group relating to this project   ❏ Yes   ❏ No

3. On an average Sunday morning, approximately how many people attend your church (including children)?
   - ❏ 150 or less
   - ❏ Between 150 and 300
   - ❏ Between 300 and 500
   - ❏ Between 500 and 1,000
   - ❏ Over 1,000

4. What denomination or affiliation is the church you currently attend?
   _____

5. How long have you been attending your present church? _____Years/_____Months

6. Was there ever a period of time in your life when you did not attend any church?
   - ❏ Yes   If yes, for how long? Years/Months_____
   - ❏ No

7. What denomination or affiliation was the church you attended while you were growing up? (If you did not attend church while you were growing up, please check "none".)
   Denomination _____ None ❏

8. Which of the following categories does your age fall into?
   - ❏ 18 or younger
   - ❏ 19-24
   - ❏ 25-34
   - ❏ 35-44
   - ❏ 45-54
   - ❏ 55-64
   - ❏ 65 or olde

9. Are you: ❏ Male   ❏ Female

10. What is your current marital status?
   - ❏ Single/Not married
   - ❏ Married
   - ❏ Divorced and remarried
   - ❏ Divorced
   - ❏ Co-habitating/Common-law
   - ❏ Separated
   - ❏ Widowed

10. What is your city and province of residence:

   City: _____   Province: _____

Thank you ...

Endnotes

FROM INTRODUCTION

1 Based on an illustration heard at a meeting in Mississauga, Ontario, by Graeme Irvine, past president of World Vision International, 1995.

2 Ronald J. Sider. *One-Sided Christianity? Uniting the Church to Heal and Lost and Broken World.* (Grand Rapids: Zondervan Publishing House, 1993), 25.

3 Jim Wallis. *The Call for Conversion* (New York: Harper, 1981), 8.

FROM CHAPTER 1

1 John Webster Grant, *The Church in the Canadian Era: The First Century of Confederation* (Toronto: McGraw-Hill Ryerson Limited, 1972), 218.

2 William H. Brackney, *Church Volunteerism* (Grand Rapids: Eerdmans, 1997), 69.

3 Phyllis D. Airhart, "Ordering a New Nation and Reordering Protestantism 1867-1914," in *The Canadian Protestant Experience 1760-1990*, George A. Rawlyk, ed. (Burlington: Welch Publishing, 1990), 101.

4 Airhart, 99.

5 Robert A. Wright, "The Canadian Protestant Tradition 1914-1945," in *The Canadian Protestant Experience 1760-1990*, George A. Rawlyk, ed. (Burlington: Welch Publishing, 1990), 101.

6 George A. Rawlyk & Mark A. Noll, *Amazing Grace: Evangelicalism in Australia, Britain, Canada, and the United States,* (Montreal & Kingston: McGill-Queen's University Press, 1994), 19.

7 Airhart, 101.

8 Kenneth Scott Latourette, *A History of Christianity, Volume II: Reformation to the Present,* (New York: Harper & Row, 1975), 1263.

9   Latourette, 1263.

10 Wright, 143.

11 Wright, 146.

12 Rawlyk & Noll, 19.

13 Mark A. Noll, *A History of Christianity in the United States and Canada,* (Grand Rapids: Wm. B. Eerdmans, 1992), 282.

14 Grant, 133.

15 Grant, 165.

16 Wright, 146.

17 Wright, 165.

18 Wright, 150.

19 Wright, 154.

20 Wright, 157.

21 Wright, 154.

22 John G. Stackhouse, Jr., "More than a Hyphen: Twentieth-Century Canadian Evangelicalism in Anglo-American Context" in *Amazing Grace: Evangelicalism in Australia, Britain, Canada, and the United States,* George A. Rawlyk & Mark A. Noll, eds. (Montreal & Kingston: McGill-Queen's University Press, 1994), 384.

23 Wright, 158.

24 Wright, 141.

25 Robert K. Burkinshaw, "Conservative Evangelicalism in the Twentieth-Century 'West': British Columbia and the United States" in *Amazing Grace: Evangelicalism in Australia, Britain, Canada, and the United States,* George A. Rawlyk & Mark A. Noll, eds. (Montreal & Kingston: McGill-Queen's University Press, 1994), 318.

26 David R. Elliott, "Knowing No Borders: Canadian Contributions to American Fundamentalism" in *Amazing Grace: Evangelicalism*

in Australia, Britain, Canada, and the United States, George A. Rawlyk & Mark A. Noll, eds. (Montreal & Kingston: McGill-Queen's University Press, 1994), 373.

27 Stackhouse, 389.

28 Stackhouse, 393.

29 Grant, 216.

30 John G. Stackhouse, Jr. "The Protestant Experience in Canada Since 1945" in *The Canadian Protestant Experience 1760-1990,* George A. Rawlyk, ed. (Burlington: Welch Publishing, 1990), 214.

31 Grant, 130.

32 Grant, 131.

33 Stackhouse, "The Protestant Experience in Canada Since 1945," 200.

34 Stackhouse, "The Protestant Experience in Canada Since 1945," 200.

35 Wright, 171.

36 Sydney E. Ahlstrom, *A Religious History of the American People: Volume 2* (Garden City: Image Books, 1975), 409.

37 Wright, 172.

38 Grant, 149.

39 Noll, 435.

40 David O. Moberg, *The Great Reversal – Evangelism versus Social Concern* (New York: J. B. Lippincott, 1972), 22.

41 Moberg, 23.

42 Wright, 189.

43 Wright, 179.

44 Wright, 180.

45 Grant, 153.

46 Wright, 190.

47 Grant, 163-164.

48 Latourette, 1455.

49 Latourette, 1454.

50 Grant, 160.

51 Grant, 160.

52 Stackhouse, "The Protestant Experience in Canada Since 1945," 200.

53 Stackhouse, "The Protestant Experience in Canada Since 1945," 206.

54 Grant, 170.

55 Grant, 161-162.

56 Noll, 438.

57 Grant, 164.

58 Grant, 166.

59 Stackhouse, "The Protestant Experience in Canada Since 1945," 201.

60 Grant, 174.

61 Stackhouse, "The Protestant Experience in Canada Since 1945," 200.

62 Grant, 174.

63 Stackhouse, "The Protestant Experience in Canada Since 1945," 203.

64 Stackhouse, "The Protestant Experience in Canada Since 1945," 204.

65 Graeme Irvine, *Best Things in the Worst Times: An Insider's View of World Vision* (Oregon: BookPartners, Inc, 1996), 17.

66 Grant, 179.

[67] Grant, 178.

[68] Grant, 178-179.

[69] Grant, 179.

[70] Ahlstrom, 600.

[71] Ahlstrom, 600.

[72] Grant, 184.

[73] Ahlstrom, 604.

[74] Ahlstrom, 603.

[75] Larry Christenson, *A Charismatic Approach to Social Action* (Minneapolis: Bethany Fellowship, 1974), 17.

[76] Ahlstrom, 608.

[77] Stackhouse, "The Protestant Experience in Canada Since 1945," 209-211.

[78] Stackhouse, "The Protestant Experience in Canada Since 1945," 209.

[79] Barbara Dafoe Whitehead, *The Divorce Culture* (New York: Alfred A Knopf, 1996), 4.

[80] Reginald W. Bibby, *Fragmented Gods* (Toronto: Irwin Publishing, 1987), 62-85.

FROM CHAPTER 2

1 William Willimon, *What's right with the Church* (San Francisco: Harper & Row, 1985), 24-25.

2 Tom Harpur, "Everyone of us walks with a limp," *The Toronto Star*, January 12, 1997.

3 Marcus J. Borg, *Meeting Jesus Again for the First Time: The Historical Jesus & the Heart of Contemporary Faith* (San Francisco: Harper Collins, 1995), 15.

4 Philip Yancey, *The Jesus I Never Knew* (Grand Rapids: Zondervan, 1995), 266.

5 Ronald J. Sider, *One-Sided Christianity? Uniting the Church to Heal a Lost and Broken World* (Grand Rapids: Zondervan Publishing House, 1993), 61.

6 C.S. Lewis (Edited by Walter Hooper), *The Business of Heaven* (Great Britain: William Collins), 17.

7 C. Kirk Hadaway and David A. Roozen, *Rerouting the Protestant Mainstream: Sources of Growth & Opportunities for Change* (Nashville: Abingdon Press, 1995), 83.

8 Karl Rahner, *The Religious Life Today* (New York: Seabury Press, 1975), 8.

9 Robert E. Logan and Larry Short, *Mobilizing for Compassion: Moving People into Ministry* (Grand Rapids: Fleming H. Revell, 1994), 11.

10 Wallis, Jim. *The Soul of Politics: A Practical and Prophetic Vision for Change* (The New Press. New York, 1994), 36.

11 Wallis, Jim. *The Soul of Politics*, 36.

12 Sider, Ronald, J. *One-Sided Christianity*, 184.

13 Robert E. Logan and Larry Short, *Mobilizing for Compassion*, 11.

FROM CHAPTER **3**

1 Jeff Woods, *Congregational Megatrends* (New York: The Alban Institute, 1996), 103.

2 Mike Regele *The Death of the Church* (Grand Rapids: Zondervam, 1995), 206.

3 Eugene Peterson, *Under The Unpredictable Plant: An Exploration in Vocational Holiness* (Grand Rapids: William B.Eerdmans Publishing Company, 1994), 14.

4 Richard Higginson, *Transforming Leadership: A Christian Approach to Management* (London: SPCK, 1996), 117.

5 Quoted by Richard John Neuhaus in *Freedom for Ministry* (San Francisco: Harper and Row, 1979), 13.

6 Susan Howatch, *Absolute Truths,* (Knopf: New York, 1995).

7 John Cougar Mellancamp song *Between a Laugh and a Tear* in the Scarecrow Album, 1994.

8 Benton Johnson, Dean R. Hoge and Donald A. Luidens, "Mainline Churches: The Reason for Decline," *First Things* (March 1993), 18.

9 William Willimon and Stanley Hauerwas, *Where Resident Aliens Live* (Nashville: Abingdon, 1996), 101.

10 Stephen Covey, *First Things First* (New York: Simon & Schuster, 1994), 74.

11 Eugene Peterson. *Under the Unpredictable Plant: An Exploration in Vocational Holiness* (Grand Rapids: William B.Eerdmans Publishing Company, 1994), 44.

12 Loren Mead. *The Once and Future Church* (New York: The Alban Institute, 1991), 53.

13 C. Kirk Hadaway and David Rozen. *Rerouting the Protestant Mainstream: Sources of Growth and Opportunities for Change* (Nashville: Abingdon Press, 1995), 88.

[14] Gordon Macdonald, *The Life God Blesses: Weathering the Storms of Life That Threaten the Soul* (Nashville: Thomas Nelson, 1994), xii.

[15] MacDonald, 216.

[16] Lee Bolman and Terence Deal, *Leading With Soul: An Uncommon Journey of the Spirit* (San Francisco: Jossey Bass, 1995), 39.

[17] Charles Van Engen, *God's Missionary People: Rethinking the Purpose of the Local Church* (Grand Rapids: Baker Books, 1991), 165.

[18] Van Engen, 166.

FROM CHAPTER 4

[1] Kennon Callahan, *Effective Church Leadership* (San Francisco: Harper and Row, 1990), 3.

[2] Lecture notes: Harold Percy, September, 1994.

[3] Michael Armour and Don Browning, *Systems Sensitive Leadership* (Joplin College Press, 1995), 217.

[4] Quoted in David Clutterbuck and Stuart Crainer, *Makers of Management: Men and Women Who 5 Changed the Business World* (London: Guildford Publishing, 1990), 190.

[5] Clutterbuck and Crainer, 217.

[6] The same leadership scale was used in the previous *Where's A Good Church?* research project. The results were almost identical.

[7] Don Posterski and Irwin Barker, *Where's a Good Church?* (Winfield, BC: Wood Lake Books, 1993), 179.

[8] Charles Van Engen, *God's Missionary People* (Grand Rapids: Baker Books, 1991), 165.

[9] Van Engen,166.

[10] Van Engen, 54.

[11] Warren Bennis and Burt Nanus, *Leaders: Strategies of Taking Charge* (San Francisco: Harper and Row, 1985), 53.

FROM CHAPTER 5

1 George Barna, Ventura: (Regal Books, 1990), 153.

2 Donald C. Posterski and Irwin Barker, *Where's a Good Church?* (Winfield, BC: Wood Lake Books, 1993), 37-40.

3 Paul Wilke, *The Good Enough Catholic: A Guide for the Perplexed* (New York: Ballantine Books, 1996), 8.

4 Paul Wilke, *The Good Enough Catholic*, xiv.

5 Schaeffer, Francis A. *The Church at the End of the Twenty-First Century* (London: Norfolk Press, 1970), 51.

6 Schaeffer, Francis A. *The Church at the End of the Twenty-First Century*, 50.

7 Walter J. Burghardt, "Justice in God's Own Book", *The Living Pulpit*, January–March 1993, 4.

8 Cited by Marcus J. Borg, *Meeting Jesus Again for the First Time: The Historical Jesus & the Heart of Contemporary Faith* (San Francisco: HarperCollins, 1995), 136.

9 William H. Willimon, *The Intrusive Word: Preaching to the Unbaptized,* (Grand Rapids: William B.Eerdmans Publishing Company, 1994), 39.

FROM CHAPTER 6

1 Carl George, *The Coming Church Revolution: Empowering Leaders for the Future* (Grand Rapids: Revel, 1994), 37.

2 Ray Bakke, *The Urban Christian* (Downers Grove: InterVarsity Press, 1989), 23.

3 Loren Mead, *The Once and Future Church* (New York: The Alban Institute, 1991), 70.

4 James Fowler, *Weaving the New Creation* (San Francisco: Harper, 1991), 151.

5 Rodney Clapp, *A Peculiar People: The Church as a Culture in a Post-Christian Society* (Downers Grove, IL: InterVarsity Press, 1996), 116.

6 William Willimon and Stanley Hauerwas, *Resident Aliens* (Nashville: Abingdon Press, 1989), 46-47.

7 Stanley Grenz, *Created for Community* (Wheaton, IL: Bridgepoint Books, 1996), 209.

8 Ronald Sider, *One-Sided Christianity* (Grand Rapids: Zondervan, 1993), 198.

9 Roger Mitchell, *The Kingdom Factor: An Introduction to Living in the Kingdom of God* (San Francisco: Marshall Pickerin, 1986).

10 Jim Wallis, *A Practical and Prophetic Vision for Change* (New York: The New Press, 1994), 71.

11 Marva J. Dawn, *Reaching Out Without Dumbing Down: A Theology of Worship for the Turn of the Century* (Grand Rapids: Eerdmans, 1995), 139.

12 Daniel Olson, "Congregational Growth and Decline in Indiana Among Five Mainline Denominations," in *Church and Denominational Growth*, ed. Roozen and Hadaway (Nashville: Abingdon Press, 1993), 221-224.

13 Jeff Woods, *Congregational Megatrends* (New York: The Alban Institute, 1996), 52.

14 A story told by Tom Sine at the Urban Conference in Chicago, 1986.

15 Alan Roxburgh, *Reaching a New Generation* (Downers Grove, IL: InterVarsity Press, 1993), 8.

16 Eddie Gibbs, *In Name Only: Tackling the Problem of Nominal Christianity* (Downers Grove, IL: InterVarsity Press, 1994), 100.

17 Jeff Woods, *Congregational Megatrends*, 20.

18 Mike Regele, *Death of the Church* (Grand Rapids: Zondervan, 1995), 203.

FROM CHAPTER 7

1 N. Timms, European Values Study, 1981-1990.

2 Stanley Hauerwas, an illustration on tape from a course he was teaching.

3 Kirk Hadaway, David Roozen, *Rerouting the Protestant Mainstream* (Nashville, Abingdon Press, 1995), 86.

4 Robert Farrar Capon, *The Astonished Heart: Reclaiming the Good News from the Lost-and-Found of Church History* (Grand Rapids: William B. Eerdmans Publishing Company, 1996), 105.

5 Peter T. Chattaway, "Regent undoes Jesus Seminar," *Christian Week*, June 24, 1997, front page.

6 Capon, *The Astonished Heart*, 92.

7 Michael Adams, *Sex in the Snow* (Toronto: Penguin Books, 1997), 12.

8 TV program, "Entertainment Tonight," April 15, 1997.

9 An excerpt from an interview on Mars Hill Tapes with Michael Sandall. Quote from his book, *Democracy's Discontent: America In Search of a Public Philosophy*, July/August 1996.

10 Adams, *Sex in the Snow*, 19.

11 Donald C. Posterski, *True to You: Living our Faith in Our Multi-Minded World* (Winfield, BC: Wood Lake Books, 1995), 62.

12 Hervé Carrier, S.J., *Evangelizing the Culture of Modernity* (New York: Orbis Books, 1993), 1.

13 William Blair Gould, *Frankl: Life with Meaning* (Kentucky: Wadsworth).

14 Archbishop of Canterbury George Carey on a visit to Egypt and Sudan. Quoted in the *Anglican Journal*.

15 Dorothy L. Sayers, *A Matter of Eternity* (Grand Rapids: William B. Eerdmans Publishing Company, 1973), 103.

[16] Philip Yancey, *The Jesus I Never Knew* (Grand Rapids: Zondervan, 1995), 267.

[17] Philip Yancey, *The Jesus I Never Knew*, 268.

[18] Mary E. Hines, *The Transformation of Dogma: An Introduction to Karl Rahner.* (New York: Paulist Press, 1989), 119.

[19] Marcus J. Borg, *Meeting Jesus Again for the First Time: The Historical Jesus & the Heart of Contemporary Faith* (San Francisco: Harper Collins, 1995), 17.

[20] C. Kirk Hadaway & David A. Roozen, *Rerouting the Protestant Mainstream: Sources of Growth & Opportunities for Change* (Nashville: Abingdon Press, 1995), 88.

[21] Mark Noll, *The Scandal of the Evangelical Mind* (Grand Rapids: William B. Eerdmans Publishing Company, 1994), 141.

[22] Ronald J. Sider, *One-Sided Christianity* (Grand Rapids: Zondervan, 1993), 181.

[23] N.T. Wright, *New Tasks for a Renewed Church*, (London: Hodder and Stoughton, 1992), 86.

[24] Ronald J. Sider, *One-Sided Christianity*, 104.

[25] J. H. Yoder, *The Politics of Jesus* (Paternoster Press, Carlisle, U.K., 1994), 246.

[26] Hervé Carrier, S.J., *Evangelizing the Culture of Modernity*, 3.

[27] Sherwood, E. Wirt, *The Social Conscience of the Evangelical* (Harper and Row, New York. 1968), 8.

[28] Note: Two of the 14 Future Faith Churches – The Meeting Place and the Chinese church – placed the least emphasis on social care. In an overall rating, The Vineyard Church was highest on both soul care and social care. The Aboriginal Pentecostal Church did not participate in this component of the survey.